Church of the Perfect God

Carl Peterson

2013
© Carl Peterson
ISBN 978-0-473-08927-6

Unit 3, #2 Hynds Road
Greerton, Tauranga
New Zealand 3112

E-mail: perfectgod@outlook.co.nz
Mobile: 64 7 21 753 693

Table of Contents

Page No.

Table of Contents

Page No.

Table of Contents

Table of Contents

Church of the Perfect God

Carl Peterson

Carl Peterson

Introduction

In 1969 I made a difficult decision that would ultimately lead me on an amazing journey of physical, mental, and spiritual self discovery. While under guard to be put on a military transport that was to take me to the war arena of Southeast Asia, I escaped out a toilet window and fled the US military to Canada as a deserter.

A two year stint in a spiritual commune in British Columbia acquainted me with an interesting meditation phenomenon: I began hearing a gentle ringing in my mind that activated my awareness and my connect-ability with others.

After the BC government issued an eviction order to the members of our commune, I moved to Nova Scotia. With a few friends, I created a modest financial nest egg by developing properties and renovating older homes.

My family and I paused for awhile in Fiji in 1974 on our way to Sydney Australia to begin a new life. A lucid dream remembered, and serendipity, led us to purchase a remote 500 acre property on the island of Vanua Levu, where we remained for the best part of the thirteen years we lived in Fiji.

I continued meditating to my 'ringing' while we built upon our Fiji dream.

The Fiji military coup of 1987 cut short our dreams and ambitions in Fiji. Neighborhood riots led by marauding Fijian youths caused me to send my family to New Zealand to wait out the coup and see what would happen to our business and property in Fiji. Soon after, because of my outspoken anti-apartheid view, I was arrested three times by the military government, and finally kidnapped and savagely beaten by armed soldiers.

In August 1987 I rejoined my family in Rotorua, New Zealand, as a political refugee, abandoning all my work, assets, and properties in Fiji. The only thing of value I was able to bring out of my Fiji experience was an idea for a unique portable sawmill that I had been toying with.

This seed became the Peterson Portable Sawmill marketed by my former company Peterson Portable Sawing Systems Ltd. After notable success between 1989 and 1996 that company was forced into receivership in early 2006 by an ungrounded patent infringement claim against PPSSL and me. The company was formally liquidated in 2007 while the court case dragged on.

Ultimately, in 2009 I won in my own defense in a case that had featured in the New Zealand Supreme Court. I continue to be engaged in the New Zealand courts as a lay litigant, seeking compensation for the loss of my company; loss of my New Zealand properties; the breakup of my family; copyright infringement against my sawmill designs; and the continuing presence of an invalid patent that encroaches upon my Intellectual Property rights.

The Peterson Portable Sawmill is now being ably manufactured by my daughter and son-in-law through Peterson Global Sales Ltd. in Rotorua.

Over the years I have perfected my meditation around the 'ringings,' and on occasion began hearing seven distinct inner vibrations that heralded an incredible feeling of overwhelming and unconditional love.

Shortly after sharing this gift at my first public presentation in early November 2010, I was diagnosed with a serious prostate cancer. Immediate and invasive treatment was strenuously advised.

I consulted my ringings and stubbornly refused any form of medical treatment. For eight months I attempted to heal my cancer through my own meditation technique. For eight months the cancer advanced alarmingly until my surgeon announced that if my PSA (prostate specific antigen) test rose any more - it was up to 20 by that time - it would probably be too late to operate, as the cancer by then might have spread to the bones.

I was led to a Maori healer who performed a mirimiri massage on me. I learned through that healer that my mother had been insane when I was three years old, and that my cancer was caused by the huge amount of anger I was harboring in and through my prostate gland.

When I heard the word insane, I felt as if I had been struck by lightning. The memory of that early experience flooded back to me. I remembered deciding that my mother was insane and that I would never, ever let her get close enough to me to abuse me again.

And I never did.

In remembering, I was able to bring my now mature understanding of the situation back to the original memory. I realized that my mother was caught up in her own arena of despair; suffering hormone imbalance, loneliness from a husband who was seldom home either emotionally or physically, and the endless strain of raising six kids more or less on her own.

I recognized that my childhood story was jaded and inaccurate. I reframed the memory from my adult understanding, and stopped blaming my mother for succumbing to the immense human pressures that bore down on her. Importantly, I stopped blaming myself for buying into a victimhood that had cursed me throughout my adult life.

One year later, the cancer is effectively gone, receding by leaps and bounds over that year. I am physically, mentally, and spiritually invigorated, and my life has taken on a new and more colorful quality.

My healing experience has led me into an amazing investigation as to why, when, and how this healing has come about.

What I have discovered amounts to an astounding new science and opens the possibility for an entirely new form of medicine. This would incorporate the best practices of spiritual development along with the best-known means of healing the emotional childhood wounds that result from the almost inevitable moments of abuse by abandonment that is commonplace within the modern family.

This sense of abuse probably begins in the birthing process itself and is only defined and accentuated by later events in infancy.

On the face of it, I have discovered why, with all our technology and luxury, it has become so difficult to connect with others. Why relationships fail time after time. Why life-threatening illnesses are often predictable and that they can be treatable without invasive surgery. Where most, if not all, mental illness originates from. Why so few of us are consciously able to access the extreme genius that lies dormant within every human mind.

And why many of us are almost universally unhappy.

Most men live lives of quiet desperation.

Henry David Thoreau

Once we discover what we are not, and set that illusion aside, we are left with what is. I have discovered this to be an incredible reflection of a perfect creation designed to bathe us in love, joy and ecstasy should we allow those divine gifts to enter our minds, our souls, and our hearts.

My personal experience in bliss opened my eyes to the reality that all *is* love, there is a perfect God and there must be a reason for all things. Everything I have learned and share in this book emanates from this realization.

And our only duties are to accept our circumstances – our karma - and surrender to that perfect love.

How easy is that?

It must be so. Nothing else makes sense.

Woven through the fabric of my existence the Creator has revealed its substance, purpose and fulfillment.

Infinity and eternity define a formless energy intent on experiencing its own beauty, wisdom and perfection - through and with us.

THE SIREN'S CALL

Sometimes I hear the sweetest voice call from far away,
It reaches me through open door and window where I lay.

A voice that speaks with different words than those I use today.
I do not know the meaning, but I cannot turn away.

But something touches deep inside and wakes me from my sleep.
As if a long lost contract has come back for me to keep.

I hear that voice each time into your naked eyes I look,
That voice is now my truth and it's the subject of this book.

I can't resist your siren's call, this magnet draws me near.
And if I can't go there to you, I have to call you here.

And so it is with you and me, in book our paths will meet.
Before too many pages turned our contract to complete.

But worry not, I don't make haste to burn what's in the pot,
I know you can't rush in until you know just what it's not.

So bide your time with me awhile and let the cooking simmer.
I understand your fear in that the ice gets ever thinner.

Just give me your attention now, this book is like a letter.
And by the time you've finished it, I hope you'll know you better.

And as you learn just who I am, and who you are to me,
You'll know you're why I've written this, the lens by which I see.

So brace yourself for what comes next it's more than just a sliver.
The story of my life in love I'm pleased to now deliver.

Part 1: Connection

I am the Universe

It is written that when the young Krishna's mother looked into his mouth, she saw the universe. I believe that the ancient scriptures are wrong. Krishna's mother saw the universe when she looked into his eyes.

This experience was beautifully depicted in The Life of Pi. Seeing this movie reminded me, once again, of who and what I am, and of the wonderful experience to be had when any two people even for a moment permit God to reveal itself in holy communication one with another.

Krishna must have had a wonderful mother; one who herself fully understood her part in the divine drama. Children already have a predisposition towards love and connection, yet it is extremely unusual for an adult to have maintained that same predisposition.

It is our relentless adherence to culture and circumstance that hides our self from ourselves, continually leading the children away from selflessness and towards careful protection of the ego, a sense of separation from the natural world and disconnection with all other people.

Who amongst us has had such a mother as Krishna's? Not I, at least, and I have heard of no other in all of history. And thus the sins of the parents are visited upon the children generation after generation. Or so it seems; it may not be so.

It might be that even as Krishna discovered his true self in a time long lost to us in the distant past, the human world was already forging the karmic lessons necessary to advance the divine human soul in all its many manifestations. And even now the world is relentlessly marching towards a new heaven on earth; a heaven on earth already available to any and all willing to complete the karmic lessons required of us that allow us to reach ultimate compassion and a resulting nirvana.

Who am I to say and who am I to know? I am simply a lone pilgrim traveling through one incarnation after another in search of my own karmic and spiritual advancement; desirous of the reward that awaits all of us.

That is, a fuller remembrance of the one true self, and the divine experience of the entire universe blessed with the amazing prize of total self-awareness.

A universe not only conscious of itself, but also able to recognize itself in all its glory; hear itself breathing creation into being; turn itself inside out in introspection; see itself in all its mystery, magic, beauty and perfection, and feel itself in oneness with itself.

I know this to be true, not from the ancient writings, but from my own personal experiences, some only temporary and fleeting, but sufficient thereof to lead me on a journey of more than sixty years in search of the other selves that might allow me to stand again within those total realizations.

In remembering we become the universe in its fulfillment.

Our shared destiny.

I remember you.

A NEW BEGINNING

Choices once obscure have now become clearer.
As cries in the wilderness draw nearer and nearer.

Fears never spoken multiplied in denial.
Anger newly vented given birth to the vile.

Neighbors never known breaking down the fences.
New-felt emotions challenging the senses.

Worries about material things, giving way to feeling.
Seeing things as they are, ego sent reeling.

A storm catching us unaware.
A tempest stripping our beliefs bare.

A calm giving us time to cope.
A coming together, reason to hope.

A warning for the days to come.
A time to choose what we will become.

Stepping beyond the past from what was before.
Daring to step forward through another door.

Embracing new reality, which joins us all as one.
Understanding all we do adds to the one great sum.

Stepping forward consciously, daring to be judged by others.
Choosing friends who share our passions, defining us as brothers.

Supporting those with heavy burdens, giving them a helping hand.
Seeing kindness slowly spreading, being cause throughout the land.

When at last we learn to listen, giving self to God's great plan.
Sharing love without condition is what it is to be a man.

Until we learn that lesson clearly, letting love within us dwell,
Nothing that we do has meaning, just another day in hell.

If we fail to learn that lesson, we will likely miss the bus.
This is just a new beginning that can only start with us.

Innocent Love

Something wonderful happened when I was eight years old, the year I was in the second grade. My best friend Dennis Robinson and I both loved the same girl, Sharon Staley. We agreed to share Sharon with each other. What this meant was, we would all three do things together.

So, every day after school we would both walk Sharon the half mile or so back to her home. We would go down into her basement, which consisted of a bare concrete floor and a single wooden support post in the middle. Dennis and I would climb aboard the two tricycles there and we would begin riding round and round the basement post. Sharon would always be the 'policeman,' and each time we passed by she would stop us and claim a kiss.

Joy of joys! Ecstasy, oh ecstasy! We laughed, we cried, we loved. We were transported to another world and into another dimension, lifted up into another state of being. We saw God. We touched God. We kissed God. We felt God. We *were* little gods having the time of our lives.

This continued for hours each day, every day after school, for weeks and weeks, and perhaps months and months. We lived for that time in the other world. Sharon's basement was the 'Stargate' and nothing else mattered.

Then one day it was gone. Sharon and her parents moved to another town. Dennis moved to another school in the same town. Nothing was ever the same again.

The experience of love faded into a distant memory of what could be, but was no more.

Except ye be converted, and become as little children, ye shall not enter into the kingdom of heaven.

Matthew 18, v 3

21

Between the ages of six to fourteen, I was sent by my parents for eight weeks during the summer vacation to Camp Aquila, a boys' camp on Star Lake near Dent, Minnesota. This camp was located on a truly beautiful wilderness retreat in the northern part of the state.

I remember the summer Sharon moved away. That year I enjoyed a special relationship with the world of nature. I took to sneaking off by myself and wandering the five hundred acres of forest in peaceful bliss, marveling at the beauty and energy of the wild. This was another magical place that spoke to me. This was the great 'I Am' calling out to me.

For weeks I had been tuning in to the forest, going deeper and deeper into my reverie. I felt I was being held and rocked by a gentle background humming sensation. Then one day I became so immersed in this experience I lost track of time, and failed to hear the assembly bells calling us in for the midday meal.

The entire camp was mobilized to find this lost child. From that day forward I was not allowed to go anywhere by myself. I was under guard for the remainder of the camp experience. Yet another connection taken away from me.

Then along came Fourth Grade when I was ten years old. We had a great teacher that year, Miss Shipley. She encouraged me to be more. She somehow inspired me to use my intuitive gifts in my schoolwork and math.

That year I was special. That year I didn't disappoint.

A good year, but also the year that small cliques began to form. The year that some of the kids became popular, and others not so popular. The great popularity contest had begun!

I was doing all right, you know. Good looking kid (apart for some weirdo teeth sticking straight out). One of the brightest, teacher's pet and all that, and hanging out with the popular kids.

One day I was exercising my freedom to be a little monster at the expense of a shy and 'not so popular' girl who sat at the desk in front of me. Her name was Diana Pence and she had gorgeous long red hair. I took a freshly-sharpened pencil and jabbed it into the back of her neck.

Still don't know why I did that. Punishment, I guess, for not being popular. And I have no idea what I expected to happen. Maybe she would bow down and acknowledge me as her master, or something. Maybe I just wanted to see her cry.

It didn't happen.

What did happen knocked the socks off me. She turned and looked at me. No anger. No tears. No words. Nothing but love.

Something seemed to pour out of her eyes into my own; and into my heart and into my soul. Magic or something; color, electricity, energy, vibration- I didn't know what. Whatever it was, it was awesome.

I was looking into God! I held that look for a few long moments and then I broke away.

I wanted to be loved by one of the popular girls; this little God wasn't good enough for me! So God turned herself around and went back to doing her homework.

Even while love searches for its reflection, the ego lurks behind as silent protector and saboteur.

Blessed are the pure of heart: for they shall see God.

Matthew 5, v.8

23

THE ANONYMOUS SMILE

The anonymous smile is delight to us all
And it's hard to resist its magical call.
It only can happen when we drop our guard,
Or when someone else plays God's wild card.

The anonymous smile is loved by so many,
It's almost like magic; the effect is uncanny
At the heart of each smile is the secret of living
That is, at its core, the spirit of giving.

And who wins the game at the end of the play?
It's he who has smiled the most you might say.
It's the thing that transports us away from our fear,
And reminds us once more that love is right here.

Awaiting the chance to be seen one more time,
Our higher self once more to define.
To remind us again of why we have come
To explore the beauty of God's one great sum.

For God has given us blindfolds at birth
To make the game fun, for what it is worth.
If there was no mystery, we might well be bored,
And that would be something the Good Lord abhorred.

God cloaks his hand with the anonymous smile
To caress and embrace us at least for awhile.
And hopes that we might be gone not so long
And instead might return to where we belong.

God covers his hand with a glove, don't you see,
And in mystery invites us towards what we must be.
You are the same smile you see in his eyes,
Wake up! You are Gods, the Good Lord cries!

Perhaps you will hide from the smile that you see,
And run from the truth of what you might be.
The truth is we can't really live in denial.
But rather, beloved, we live in God's smile.

Stranger in a Strange Land

My sophomore year in high school (tenth grade, at age sixteen) I was doing pretty well in sports. I made the first team in basketball and football (gridiron), and lettered in varsity track and field. One afternoon after I had excelled in a tenth grade intra-city football match, the varsity coach invited three of us precocious tenth graders up to practice with the twelfth grade team.

I was put in on defense as a linebacker. The first play of the scrimmage (practice, as in a live game), the ball carrier and two blockers came straight at me. I lowered my head, planted my feet, and hoped for the best. At contact I felt a sharp pain at the back of my neck, and then everything went black. Moments, or minutes, later when I regained consciousness, I was flat on my back.

I quickly jumped up, somehow knowing what I was to do, and determined to hold my ground. Play after play came my way. No one got through. I was quick. I was alert. I was fearless. I was absolute 'death' to the boy with the ball.

Forty-five minutes later the head coach called me over.

"Peterson, come over here. What's got into you?"

I didn't know who Peterson was. I didn't know who the coach was. I didn't know who I was. All I knew at that moment was the game. No memory, no expectation, no 'looking good,' no fear. Just stop the guy with the ball. I was totally present. That's all it takes to be great. That's all it takes. All you've got to do is get your mind out of the way.

Sounds simple, doesn't it?

They rushed me up to the locker room. Which locker was mine? Somehow someone opened my locker. Called my mother in. Here's me naked in the shower and this unknown and eccentric lady rushes in! Weird stuff.

Things got stranger and stranger. My family and the other people in my life were all hiding behind masks. They weren't being honest. They were acting out some petty delusion, some sort of pretense.

And me a stranger in a strange land. A stranger in my own home.

I saw it all.

I sought out a private place in my home, where I slowly began to come to grips with these new sensations, and began to enjoy the same gentle humming I had experienced in the forest when I was younger. With the humming came an absolute clarity in being present; in living in the moment.

Those moments became precious and priceless.

Then I waited, dreading the return of memory, and that all-obscuring cloud of mind chatter which seemed to accompany it. Some other power, it seemed, was trying to reclaim its position of power and authority over me. Was this my ego, the false identity that we humans seem to be forever buying in to? Quietly it came in, little by little, like a thief in the night. I felt myself powerless to resist. I returned to the addiction of memory kicking and screaming, gnashing my teeth against the presumed inevitable. But I had seen what clarity of thought and being was possible. And in some deep place within me I shifted slightly the rudder of my being.

So I fought my way, on a mental level, through high school. Going to college released me from some of the old rules, but brought new rules as well. Harder rules.

Work harder. Learn faster. Prepare yourselves for the battle of the boardroom. Or else give yourself up for a little country in South East Asia called Viet Nam; a new little paradise for those who create the world's money supply through debt, and profit through the sale of arms.

I drank heavily in my three years of college and university study. I didn't want to be there. I wasn't ready to learn anything. But neither did I want to go to somebody else's war.

Of that I was certain.

I finally made a total break from what was expected of me, and enrolled in Orange Coast Junior College in Costa Mesa, California. Goodbye, the Midwest. Goodbye, Iowa.

I loved the weather. I loved the freedom of California. I loved skipping classes. I experimented with drugs. Marijuana, hashish, mescaline, LSD, maybe some others, too. The one positive thing that came out of those experiences was the ever-renewing realization that consciousness is not a fixed commodity, and things may not be what they seem. One drink, one joint, one consciousness expanding event, is all it takes to realize this, and I had already had plenty. With drugs it's so easy. Pop a pill and you're there.

Somewhere else.

No work at all.

Curiously, with the drugs came a taste of the old buzz experienced on rare occasions earlier in my life. Pot, especially, seemed to dull the mental chatter enough to hear and feel the buzz. I enjoyed it while it lasted - and it didn't.

When you rely on drugs, you don't know where you are. You can be anywhere. You're not the driver. The drug takes you too often to the very place you do not want to go. The place you're not ready for.

I wasn't ready. LSD nearly destroyed me. I failed all my classes.

Why did I drink, take drugs, and continually try to escape from my supposed reality? Looking back on it now, it is apparent that I was always confronted with an inner conflict regarding who I was. Sometimes I felt worthless within my own skin, and incapable of ever amounting to anything.

And other times it seemed that the world was conspiring to ensure I always remained a victim. The drink and the drugs were a way of dulling the pain resulting from that inner conflict. Might this be the reason anyone succumbs to the comfort of alcohol, tobacco, and other intoxicating drugs? I think we go there to escape the pain of our own unresolved childhood torments.

Then I got my Army draft notice in the mail. Had to go home and say goodbye. I didn't want to go, but there seemed no other choice. I certainly wasn't in a powerful place for making choices.

Army training was my worst nightmare. I felt it was a continuing battle between my own conscience, and the desire to surrender to others and be given some sort of temporary peace.

After four weeks of basic training, I was almost ready to give in. Then we were given a one hour furlough to go to the base bar and pub as a reward for our hard training. I've never seen so much beer consumed by so few, so fast. After an hour of guzzling, we somehow managed to drag ourselves back for our company formation and roll call.

The drill instructor sergeant called out our line numbers. We, then, were to call out our last name, first name and, 'Here, Drill Sergeant.' A dozen or more numbers were called, and replied to. The company was falling back into submission, fear, and the serious business of death and killing.

Finally my line number was called: 'Number 125?'

There was a brief pause while I gathered my courage, and my resolve. Finally, I replied, "Bingo, Drill Sergeant!"

Pandemonium broke out amongst the ranks. The tension was irretrievably broken. Uncontrollable laughter and relief engulfed the entire company. I was so overcome with joy, relief and laughter that I couldn't stand. The drill sergeant attempted to regain control and order for two hours before the company was finally dismissed back to the barracks. In that time I achieved a personal high of two thousand press-ups, as the DI tried to subdue my mirth.

After that experience, I knew that I was still free, at least in my mind. I bent the rules as much and as often as I could. Each minor mental victory renewed my hope of remaining my own person; marching to my own drumbeat.

During the army experience I applied for Conscientious Objector (CO) status several times. CO status would have allowed me to serve without carrying a gun. But because I had no formal religious doctrine or support group, it was always denied. I guess I was the perfect cannon-fodder type army trainee. Finally, I was given orders for South East Asia. Korea, at least at first.

I took a stand. I told my commanding officer that I would not ship out without CO status. He left me in his office to think for thirty minutes, in the hope I would change my mind. For the first time in my life, I needed to know if there was a god, or something that might make sense of this mess I had got myself into.

So I prayed. I asked. I begged. I demanded. I pleaded. Hello? Is anything out there? For around twenty minutes into this exercise nothing happened. Finally I decided to listen. Just listen, for a change.

A strange and wonderful feeling came over me. Like being gently washed over by a humming vibration of love and compassion. Words seemed to form in my mind.

"Don't be afraid. I love you. They can't hurt you. You are a spirit. Do what is right."

But when ye pray, use not vain repetitions, as the heathens do; for they think that they shall be heard for their much speaking.

Matthew 6, v.7

When my captain returned, I was even more resolved in my stand. I expected to be sent to military prison. To my surprise, the captain ordered two sergeants to dress me in my class A travelling uniform and, forcibly, if necessary, to put me on the midnight transport plane to Korea. Like Pontius Pilate, he was washing his hands of his involvement with me.

We were waiting for the bus to the plane in an office. Five minutes before the bus was to arrive, I was allowed into the office toilet. Miraculously, there was an open window above the basin.

For a moment, I hesitated. What would it be like if I went out that window? Would I be safe? Would I ever be safe again? Then the question changed.

Would I be *free?*

I felt a sense of freedom begin to creep over me. I could do this. The thought of freedom smothered my fears.

I went for it.

Within thirty seconds I was out the window and into the night. The moment my dangling feet touched the ground in the darkness outside of the building, I knew I *was* free. Everything changed in that single moment. I would never go back.

I *could* never go back.

I guess, in a way, *no one* can ever go back.

For most, that is a difficult and powerful truth to accept. The past is gone. All that remains is the present and the infinite possibilities for the future. It was easier for me than most. I didn't have any other choice but to go forward.

Three days later I found myself in Vancouver, British Columbia, Canada, along with thousands of other American draft dodgers and deserters.

Just as in the physical realm, there is a powerful inertia at work compelling us to continue in our prevailing emotional direction.

This emotional inertia manifests in our lives as habit; often requiring risk, energy and effort in order to turn things around.

If I hadn't changed my direction I would have wound up where I was going.

...a prophet hath no honor in his own country.

John 4, v.44

SAFE OR FREE

Once a small bird flew over to me,
And asked, for a while, to perch in my tree.

In fact, to be honest; (and I'm trying to be),
There's been more than one, perhaps two or three.

They all have been different; I've had some great fun,
But some things they shared, so I'll talk like they're one....

She'd lived in a cage, for most of her life,
To children a mother, to husband a wife.

In fine sunny weather, she was my delight,
But in thunder and lightning she often took flight.

Returned to the cage that remained in her mind;
To comfort and safety, a place not unkind.

One day she didn't return to my tree,
And sometimes I wonder just where she might be.

I hope she has not returned to her cage,
Or found another, with which to engage.

Because when she flew up so high in the sky,
She resembled an angel to my humble eye.

What a loss it would be if she flew not again,
The sunshine would lose, and the storm clouds would win.

For comfort and safety, they have their appeal,
But without passion, they just are not real.

And now I must ask, for reply then from you,
There are many who wonder, just as I do,

The question is this, please answer for me,
'Is it best to be safe, or best to be free?'

The Sideras Commune

For a year or so in Canada I struggled, trying to be someone else. Being free didn't seem to alter my lifestyle choices: all fun and no responsibility. The year was 1971. My wife Kathleen had left me and my young daughter Kerris after an uncomfortable LSD experience on our forested property.

Enough was enough.

A week later she returned for Kerris, announcing that she was going to live with the Sideras commune on Lasqueti Island, British Columbia. Graciously she invited me to accompany her and take a look for myself. I went, curious at what it was that seemed to have made such an impression on Kathleen.

The commune had originally been established to test the teachings of Jesus outside the context of the Bible. Particularly, to learn how to talk to God as Jesus reportedly did two thousand years ago. The process in the commune was a little ad hoc. People would go out in the woods by themselves and simply ask and listen. 'Asking' was little more than asking the will of the divine in that moment.

Mostly it was listening, and trying to differentiate between true revelation and our own mind's chatter. Amazingly, people seemed to be hearing the same things; that we were all a part of a divine consciousness and here to love and be loved. The message was always incredibly simple. The process opened doors and moved people beyond their belief systems.

Curiously, many persons at the commune began to hear a gentle, or not so gentle, ringing in the silence of their minds; and often the ringing was followed by a sense of revelation or divine message directed personally to that individual.

For a week I observed all of this occurring around me, wondering what it was that I was missing. I became aware that there was some kind of connective glue around the core group;

even some kind of wordless and soundless language that I was not a party to.

There were moments when I was sorely tempted to run like hell away from the place as so many other hippy visitors usually did, once they figured out no drugs were used or allowed in the commune, and that something weird and unusual was going on.

One whole night I lay awake trying to get to the bottom of the mystery. In desperation I finally began listening beyond my thoughts, and I began to be aware of a sort of whooshing energy coming through my mind, around and between my thoughts. The space in my mind seemed to expand to include a kind of infinite and eternal ocean of buzzing silence; a kind of celestial white noise. I finally realized it was a kind of ringing sound that must be exactly what the others had been experiencing.

That morning upon rising I went outside my tent and witnessed an extraordinary new perception. A monarch butterfly floated nearby me, sunlight filtering through its wings and casting golden reflections across the ground beneath. I was astounded by the perfection and intentionality of the experience. I felt as though I had never before seen such a butterfly, and such beauty.

Where had I been?

Had I been blind up to that very moment in time?

As I passed the meeting hall tent to collect breakfast for my family, my eyes met one of the founders, George Orton, and I realized immediately that we were seeing one another in a special new way that was quite out of the ordinary. We were perceiving some sort of divine energy in that passing glance that felt a lot like love. There was a deep sense of 'knowing' held within that glance. This was the secret glue that held the Sideras commune together. And in its welcoming embrace, I felt, at least for a few moments, that I was complete, whole, and worthy of the love that I was experiencing.

A few wonderful memories from my childhood flooded through my mind; memories of the moments when I had truly experienced love within a general desert of loneliness. This was part of the same thread that was somehow being stitched throughout my life. This was truly exciting stuff.

Where was it coming from?

Magic happened when I surrendered my beliefs. By asking the divine will and allowing that I didn't even know what the question was, I created a space wherein the divine spirit could speak directly through me and to me. The questions came, along with a deeper connection to the divine spirit within. I was then able to apply the infinite intelligence of my own higher self with which to answer 'our' question.

I have since learned to trust the divine spirit explicitly, but my insights do not come as unquestionable fact; rather, as 'must be so' rationality. Who or what could be more rational than the divine spirit of creation?

I committed totally to the community. A week later I went back to Courtenay on Vancouver Island to sell our property so that the commune could purchase a former missionary boat in order to begin shifting to a much bigger property two hundred miles north on Calvert Island, British Columbia. Amazingly, I was able to sell our 21-acre property within three days. The boat was purchased, and within two months the entire commune community had been relocated to Calvert Island.

My ringing came and went as if it had a mind of its own. Sometimes I seemed to be with the group, and sometimes I seemed to be an outsider looking in.

Then one night I was sitting at a picnic table within the mess tent having a hot drink. Angus Cherrington, another relatively new member sat quietly across from me. We shared the usual visual acknowledgment common in the community as we made eye contact.

Suddenly, an incredible energy passed between us flowing back and forth from within our eyes. Then the universe opened between us, and we witnessed the cosmos in its fullness and entirety, exploding, swirling, expanding, glowing, and glistening with beauty, intelligence, mystery, and magic.

We witnessed the birth and destruction of stars, solar systems and entire galaxies. We were given the answers to every question. We understood atomic power, magnetism, gravity, light and vibration.

We became that upon which we looked.

We were the universe experiencing itself.

And in that moment we understood the purpose of all life, our ultimate destiny as human beings, and the absolutely incredible gift we were to ourselves and to life. We were so full of magic that nothing was impossible, and all things could be manifested simply upon our word.

We became, together, a mutual reflection of the ONE SOUL from which we have all emerged. And in that experience we merged once again, all the while being able to see that from which we came, that which we had become, and all that we could be. This was the ultimate clairvoyant experience.

It felt to me as if the ONE SOUL had found a sort of temporary but eternal completion or fulfillment in this experience.

After a short time we returned to our former selves. We congratulated each other in wonder for being permissive enough to open that multidimensional conduit as we did. And since that moment I have been forever seeking and rekindling that sacred place in my own human relationships.

In the years since, I have had fleeting glimpses of that experience - never quite so profound or deep - but nevertheless magical in the exchange and reflection of energy. And I have come to understand how rare and precious such experiences are.

In all of history, the story of Krishna's mother seeing the universe in his mouth is the only other similar account I have ever heard of, short of my own experiences as a child.

There are many things in this life that have been withheld from us. And there are many things that we have simply been oblivious to through multi-generational forgetfulness and age-long ignorance. In being reminded of this experience of the merging of souls by seeing the Life of Pi, I realize that distinguishing this potential is part of my life journey, so that I can help all of humanity move closer towards the time when we can manifest heaven on earth. Not only as an individual experience, but as how humankind goes about its particular business of living in love, remembrance and grace. This is my call to love in forgetfulness. It's time to come out and play.

When we allow love to manifest within us there is no space big enough to contain it around us.

THERE IS A PLACE...

There is a place inside of me that calls from time to time.
It wakes me from my slumber with a ringing in my mind.

And as I listen to that sound, a symphony emerges.
A harmony of energy and love that just converges.

I step into that place I hear and choose it for my own.
Each time I go, I spend more time, it's like a second home.

One day, I know, I will not leave, but shall decide to stay.
This other place inside me is my path, it is my way.

Whenever I am feeling blue and wondering who I am,
I only need to turn around and go inside again.

For that is where my soul resides, complete in every way.
Just waiting for the chance to merge, to know another day.

God's song is always playing in the background, don't you see?
You've only got to listen up and then you will be free.

For as we open door to self and let the moment in,
The moment shares its bliss with us, and both of us then win.

God cannot see itself, my friend, without our eyes and ears;
It always takes us three to dance throughout eternal years.

In Search of Grace

We are surrounded by chaos, violence, disorder, abuse, hatred, poverty and fear. We are constantly reminded by and surrounded by evidence of what we are not.

It is not easy to remain aloof from that which we observe around us. It is not easy to consider that within and around it all there is a perfect order and reason for all things.

The Christian Bible doesn't make it any easier. Found between the front and back covers of the Bible lay enough contradictions to fill an entire set of encyclopedias. It is not difficult to imagine why so many Christian sects are at odds with other sects; even to the point of violence and massacre. And it is not difficult to see the quandary facing modern Christians.

If God is a perfect God, why then all the suffering and misery we see all around us? Christian and other religious theologians ask of us that we proceed in faith and hope that all is as it should be, and that above all human understanding, God's plan for the world is unfolding exactly as it should.

And then the same theologians exhort us to consider their particular understanding of mayhem to be the divine and eternal truth; again, simply on faith and hope. Some have advocated religion by force, such as the Christian Crusaders; or the modern Islamic Jihadists intent on 'cleansing the world' of non-believers and infidels.

Is this an expression of the love of a perfect God? Doesn't look like it, does it? One might even question whether God loves us at all.

From the very beginning of known human history, and throughout the Christian era, people have been searching for the glue that might hold relationships, families, communities and nations together; and might overcome the apparent forces of evil that seemed to be forever separating and dividing those same elements.

There is one element that seems to be universal among all the various Christian sects; and indeed inherent in most widely practiced religions. It is the concept of 'Grace' wherein one Christian or religious adherent acquires the means to see and be seen in a new and holy light.

Grace descends upon the new Christian only after he or she accepts forgiveness for sins of the past and opens their hearts to the divine essence of creation.

Forgiveness doesn't need to come by the hand of a priest, a religion or a doctrine. At its core, forgiveness is about personally letting go of the past. God can forgive us as much as she wants, but if we ourselves don't let go of our guilt we remain trapped by the past and oblivious to God's Grace in the moment.

The moment.

That's all there is - and it's the only place where Grace can exist.

Even forgiveness itself is only a half-way house to absolution. So long as we believe there is something terrible that has been done to us – or we have done to another requiring our forgiveness - we are not fully home. We must let go of every last remnant of blame – and of guilt.

Our own source within has orchestrated all our own choices, and all the karmic lessons we face. Those who bring our karmic challenges are simply messengers sent by God to hurry along our own - and their - spiritual journey. Once we accept that, it is far easier to release any and all sense of blame directed towards the messengers. Our own sense of guilt, worthlessness, and outward blame is what prevents us from experiencing Grace.

Grace can be experienced in diverse ways. As in my wonderful experience in the commune, it can be experienced clairvoyantly on a visual level. I call this experiencing Grace through the ONE SOUL of God.

In this visual connection we can feel love expressing into and out of our heart as well as our eyes.

It can be experienced in a one on one moment with our own divine mind during private meditation. I achieve this while listening to my inner ringings. Somehow I am able to express with my hearing and feel the vibrations of love in my listening. I call this experiencing Grace through the ONE MIND of God.

And it can be experienced in sacred and intimate communion when we forget ourselves and merge physically one with another. There is a deeper 'feelingness' in touch that extends far beyond the actual physical connection. I call this experiencing Grace through the ONE BODY of God, or also the ONE HEART of God.

It has been my experience that Grace is not a phenomenon exclusive to Christianity. I believe it is a natural state attainable by all persons regardless of race, religion, creed, culture or upbringing. However, the adherence to any particular religious or spiritual doctrine can place an almost insurmountable barricade between man and his divine essence.

The depth of our Grace is directly proportional to the degree to which we free ourselves from the torments of our past choices and the chains of our past belief systems. In order to embrace the eternal vibrations of the here and now we need to let go of all else.

Nor does it matter how we do that. It doesn't matter what religion or discipline we have used. It doesn't matter what we call God. It only matters that we do call and then create a space within ourselves from which God can express through us. We create the God space simply by accepting that we know nothing, that our past is nothing more than a story written by us, and that we are worthy of forgiveness no matter how that story reads.

In accepting Grace we anoint ourselves with self-worth, lovability, compassion and the ability to love deeply and unconditionally.

Through love, we learn to be cause in the experience of loving. This is connection in its purest form.

Grace.

That which flows into our emptiness even when we are not looking.

Love.

That which we experience when we listen, look and embrace the feelings that accompany the vibrations of creation.

THE WELL

I dipped into my well today,
To drink my peace of mind.
No sooner had I raised my cup,
New insight did I find.

No matter how much we take out,
The well is always brimming.
No matter just how big our cup
The well is always winning.

So then I jumped into the well,
The whole me, boots and all.
I thought I'd hit the bottom soon,
To end my chosen fall.

But just as I perceived an end,
My plan to swim back up;
The bottom moved, and I passed through,
To still a deeper cup.

And every time I'd reached the end,
And thought I'd stand no more,
A voice then came to me and said,
'There's more here to explore.'

So further down into the well,
I let myself be taken.
And each step down into these depths,
I felt myself awaken.

I live here now, within this well,
Immersed in peace of mind.
And in this place I've found God's grace,
To journey with mankind.

No battles here to win or lose,
There's nothing to be done.
When we surrender self to God,
That's when we know we've won.

Connection. Belonging. Isn't that what we're all after?

Our life began safely ensconced within a warm and nourishing womb. All our needs were met. We didn't need to think. Nobody told us what to do, how to do it, or where to do it. We didn't need to agree or disagree. We did what we felt like doing and there was no right or wrong.

Then, as we became more and more conscious - that we *were* conscious - our world began to expand beyond our means to accept and understand it. We began to be aware of our limbs, and our ability to move within the womb, without understanding where we were, what we were or why we were.

One fateful day it happened. An irresistible force came to bear upon us forcing us out from our place of comfort and solitude into a bright, loud and perplexing nether world. And nothing has been the same since.

One minute we seemed to have everything. The next minute we seemed to have nothing. Our connection, which seemed ageless and eternal, was utterly and completely transformed; seemingly gone. And there we were, ignorant, powerless, completely alone, and abandoned by whatever it was that was running the show.

We knew not from where we had come.

We knew not where we would go.

And we had no idea what the dazzling lights, the commotion of sounds and the moving figures and shapes around us meant. We were indeed entirely at the mercy of the Gods; or whatever it was that newly surrounded us.

We had emerged into 'life' from within the eternal and infinite silence and emptiness; the source of all. Within that other place we were totally and completely connected to the great Alpha and Omega. Within the ethereal spirit realm where all things are connected beyond time and space, we truly belonged.

We were one with all karma, one with all time, one with all movement, and one with all feeling.

Our journey from absolute connection to absolute separation lasted approximately nine months, the period of our gestation within the womb. This was a vast spiritual distance covered in a brief space of time.

We had come from a place of infinite connection to one of seemingly no connection. If we had any means to understand at all we were likely outraged at this unilateral change of circumstances; and devastated by an accompanying sense of abandonment. We didn't know it at the time, but sooner or later we would be returned to from where we had come by the divine hand.

In the meantime we had an incredibly challenging riddle to work out that had arrived without an instruction manual or boarding instructions.

We had purchased the ticket but forgotten which bus to take.

And no man hath ascended up to heaven, but he that came down from heaven, even the Son of Man which is in heaven.

John 3, v.13

COMPLETION

We die to knowing when we're born.
In life we rise above forgetfulness to experience self
apart from self.

What is death, but rejoining our separate selves unto
the one great Self?

So, rejoice at each new death in birth.
Rejoice at each remembering shared.
Rejoice at each rebirth in death.

The soul, perhaps in loneliness and separation, returns home.

Connection:
What is it & how do we find it?

Throughout our life, connection can strike at any time and usually when we least expect it. It can happen in the middle of a quiet meditation when we suddenly realize the presence of our own God within. It can happen spontaneously in the middle of an intimate physical relationship. Or suddenly, and for no apparent reason, our eyes will lock on another person seeing us seeing them. Some sort of magical exchange takes place. Some empty place in our heart is touched and at least momentarily filled.

This excites us.

For a while we feel loved and complete. Perhaps we take a chance and dare to love; it's natural and automatic. That's where we've come from. That's *why* we have come 'from'. If another person is involved with our 'connection,' this other person, in the beginning, gives us exactly what we think we need. They shower us with the missing love, and we shower them with 'our' love. We describe our self as 'being in love'.

Being in love is a wonderful experience. Isn't this what everyone is looking for? There is no greater truth than this: loving, and being loved in return, are our only real reasons for being. Everything else amounts to nothing more than crude stage props, costume jewelry, and the masks people wear in order to hide their own anxiety, fear, confusion and quiet desperation.

Ironically, when we go looking for love outside of ourselves we seldom find it. If we're really lucky, love finds us. And if we're really, really lucky, we recognize and honor love when it crosses our paths. For the majority, it's all about luck. Some get lucky and experience love several times during their lives.

Others get only a fleeting glimpse of love as it disappears over the horizon, while they are left wondering what happened.

Why?

Because love is something that flows outwardly from within us or scarcely at all. The harder and longer we look for love outside of ourselves, the more unlikely it becomes that we will ever fully experience it within ourselves.

Accept and you shall have. Give of your heart and you shall have even more.

THE REASON FOR BEING

There's but one reason then to be,
All else fails the test, you see.
While love reveals this truth to you,
Its absence leaves much work to do.

Where there's no love life seems morass
And even money brings no class
To hide the pain of emptiness
Or dull the curse of loneliness.

When I love you and you love me
The universe will then decree,
Fulfillment in its highest form
Instead of fear which is the norm.

We can connect in several ways,
And if we do, love always stays
To comfort us when resolve sways
And bless us both in all our days.

Through body, mind, and soul we meet
And through each one it is quite sweet,
For God to see itself in you
Or touch your soul before we're through.

There's nothing more than loving now,
It's love our mantle doth bestow,
Love is the journey and the way
To be the Christ each passing day.

The Common Human Experience

Love, the real us, is never very far away. We slip into the real 'us' all the time; whenever we stop thinking, judging, comparing, worrying, needing, wanting, fretting, or trying to fix life in some way. We usually don't experience it for long. A moment here, and a moment there. A brief pause between one thought and another, or between one musical score and another. And when we do, we seldom notice.

It's all too familiar. So familiar that we don't even distinguish the fact that something else is happening when nothing is happening. That's the silence, the source of our real being-ness, and the canvas upon which all experience is painted. And we stopped dipping into that wellspring of real substance so long ago that we've forgotten that there was anything to forget.

And that's precisely why it's so easy to fall in love. Because love is always there within us longing to be seen, heard, touched, felt and accepted.

There's a million ways to fall in love. We can fall in love in the supermarket or at the movies, at the workplace or at play, in laughter or in sadness, when all is well, or when everything is falling to bits.

We can fall in love with our best friend, or our best friend's partner. We can fall in love with our worst enemy.

Sooner or later everybody falls in love at least once. It's part of the game. We rejoice in this connection without knowing or understanding what it is, how it came to be, or how to maintain it.

And in most cases, sooner or later we lose it without ever really understanding anything about it.

The real challenge is to *stay* in love. That's where everything usually falls apart. It doesn't happen all at once. It happens by degrees. The 'disappearing connection' seems to be deeply ingrained in Western culture. In America fully 50% of all marriages fail sooner or later.

Why? There are actually at least two distinct and profound reasons why we habitually fall out of love. Love doesn't fall away from us. We fall away from love. Choice: that by which we decide not to love.

Loss of Trust

The first is because of the loss of this elusive connection (love) which is thought to be found within some other person and accessed through them.

Something inside of us tells us that we really aren't worthy of love, that this other person sooner or later will abandon us as all others have done before, that he or she does not really mean what is said, or simply that he or she will not fulfill their 'promise'.

A part of us waits, in expectation, for this to occur. Sooner or later something gets in the way, and either we or the other person encounters some special need that the opposite partner is either unwilling or unable to perceive or provide.

Each partner has entered the relationship in the belief and trust that all their emotional needs will be met by the other person.

When that fails for any reason, something in the relationship breaks down. We drop the ball, so to speak, and continue to expect to be loved; even demand to be loved, without fulfilling the other person's needs.

Each partner then feels that they have been let down, abandoned, or deserted; exactly as expected.

Trust falls away, carrying the love with it.

They no longer love us, so what is the point of carrying on? We lose trust in our partner, and lose more trust in ourselves. The connection disappears, and soon both parties begin looking for another connection outside of the original relationship.

If I trust myself and be my word within that trust, others will trust me.

Love begins there.

Without trust, the equation fails.
Language.
The mathematics of the heart.

RELATIONSHIP, EXPECTATION & TRUST

Relationship is based on trust,
That's all there is, you see.
That you will always be 'yourself'
And always I'll be 'me.'

To be ourselves in honesty
Without our past intruding:
To listen for the love each holds,
In judgments, not excluding.

We build our trust by little things
We do to honor others.
By being true upon our word
Our friends become our brothers.

Love is, of course, around us all
Awaiting its expression.
It's trust in right relationship
Helps overcome depression.

An expectation made for you
By words which I might say;
I'd better 'be my word' or else
There may be Hell to pay.

For if we fail to be our word
With others, trust is lost.
With trust goes any love we held;
Trust gone, at what a cost!

Repressed Childhood Feelings & Emotions

The second reason why love fails is far more insidious, subtle and hidden from our inquiring verbal mind. When we were born, long before we gained mastery over the world of words, our entire language was one of feelings.

Our birthing experience was based upon feelings; and we created stories around the experience and the feelings that accompanied it.

Unfortunately, those stories came forth from a place of no real understanding about what was going on around us. We were helpless, needy, and vulnerable. And after the fact of our birth, by and large our needs were met only on a minimal basis.

Most of us survive our childhood years only by the narrowest of margins. We suffer recurring abandonment in many forms, deprivation of our basic emotional needs, enumerable illnesses and accidents, and a deluge of self-perpetrating stories meant to enroll us in the lies required to sanction and support the culture and belief systems within which we are raised.

Our culture, whatever it is, describes a make-believe world that separates us from our true selves. Nothing in life is as it appears to be. Unfortunately, in order to survive and thrive in this new environment, we are forced to learn to accept the life we are given; and we really do not have any other choice but to begrudgingly adapt to our circumstances whatever they may be.

That doesn't make them or the stories we create about them true.

Being a baby is awkward. We can't do anything by ourselves. We are totally reliant on others, our caregivers. And, for the most part, they are too busy surviving in their own world of illusion to give us the care and attention we need and deserve.

So, in the absence of any understanding, and at some point very early in our childhood we come to the conclusion that we are bad little boys or girls who actually deserve even less than we get. And because it seems dangerous to even voice our disapproval at our lot, we invariably begin internalizing our emotions to one degree or another.

On the one hand, our child mind intuitively believes that we deserve exactly what we get; that our abandonment at birth and thereafter is just what we deserve. And on the other hand, the first hint of reason begins to tell us that we are simply innocent victims. And so, mixed in with the abandonment and guilt, we carry repressed anger and confusion about our lot.

These unexpressed, unresolved emotions settle somewhere in our body or in our ethereal/magnetic body field in the form of a non-verbal memory, or as a sort of inter-dimensional time warp, always waiting for another similar emotional event to occur during which the original un-expressed and/or un-resolved emotion can rise up demanding to be sorted out; usually overwhelming us without us even knowing from where or whence it came.

We almost invariably shy away from these events and try to distance ourselves from anything, anyplace, or any person likely to trigger these old emotions once again.

Unfortunately, that is a self-defeating process that only ensures that the emotional baggage remains to haunt us again and again until such time as we decide to accept and experience the emotion fully; or remember the foundational experience in all its subtle forms, re-member and reframe the experience through the eyes of the now mature 'us' or our spiritual mentor, and stop blaming all the persons who were involved at the time.

By journeying through this process we can learn to stop blaming our child self for putting this scenario in place. The coping mechanism we put in place then ensured that our soul would survive to fight and live another day; and that the internalization of our emotional experiences was actually a very effective coping mechanism to deal with the apparent absence of love and caring that we experienced.

Those unexpressed and repressed emotional feelings manifest later in our lives as a general sense of confusion about who and what we are, a low self worth, the inability to express our emotions, an abandonment mentality, innocent and/or jealous rage, unaccountable anger, poverty consciousness, a wide range of phobias and manias, and generally self-destructive behavior.

Ultimately, if these emotions are left unresolved, and major similar shock traumas occur in our adult lives, the new traumas trigger the old trauma feelings to interfere in the healing and replication process in the affected cells and organs of our body. Often this process leads to the development of life threatening cancers, challenging mental dysfunctions and a host of other diseases.

The first step towards healing is to realize that every story we created about our childhood is colored, slanted and redundant when compared to our present understanding in the now. Before we as adults can begin to actually know anything about our real spiritual selves, we need to seriously consider that our entire belief system may indeed be a house of cards comprised of emotional and intellectual blackmail.

Before we can find the source of the truth and consequently experience it, we need to surrender up everything that we think we know; even that by which we have till now defined ourselves. Somehow we need to start over, or become reborn in the Christian sense. That is why it is so important to pray and meditate from a position of complete emptiness, accepting that we don't even know what the real question is.

To be truly free in the moment requires us to be free of our past. The resulting Grace can come simply as a divine gift through faith and belief, or as a reward for clearing our karma through emotional acceptance and deeper understanding.

Holding on to the 'good' aspects of our past identity is just as restrictive and confining as is the unresolved emotional traumas of our childhood. The 'good' of circumstances is usually relied upon by the ego to compare and separate ourselves by and from others. This competitive approach to life separates us from our higher selves just as surely as our own limiting self-judgments do.

When we worship our past, it enslaves us.

Enlightenment begins when we finally accept that we don't even know where to start.

TO KNOW MYSELF COMPLETELY...

To know myself completely is to know I do not know.
I cannot truly know a place or time until I go.
My memories tend to keep me in a place that seems confused.
To give my memories meaning keeps the now with past infused.

The present keeps on changing, but these changes never last.
So there's nothing to be known 'bout the present from the past.
We needn't sort through memories to choose the good and bad.
It's all passed by and gone for now; *no reason to be sad.*

Past memories tend to keep me in a place that I've passed by.
Perhaps that's what it's like if we don't live before we die.
To grasp at fleeting memories seems a waste of precious time.
When I am truly present now the moment is sublime.

So loose your hold on what you know, and let it drift away.
It won't go far, you may have use for it another day.
But let it stay outside of self, and hold an empty cup.
Just toss your petty beliefs aside, and God will fill you up.

You see, you're not your memories; you're not what you have done.
That's only entertainment, just another old rerun.
So do not judge the present by the feelings of before.
Allow the possibility that life may offer more.

Emotions are those feelings plus a lot of extra stuff.
Our judgments from the past that make a perfect thing seem rough.
Those feelings came *from judgments when we didn't understand.*
We choose our own *experience, and not some other man.*

It is our *choice how we respond to our emotion's song.*
To back our beliefs, or to concede that we may have it wrong.
There is but one true feeling, have it less or have it more.
To know that you are love itself, you've bought the whole darned store!

I know within I do not know, *so now my mind can rest.*
Accepting I know nothing is the moment I am blessed.

Relationship Heartbreaks

Nearly all of us hold within us some aspect of our unresolved childhood traumas. This game probably wouldn't be as much fun if we didn't. In fact, one of the greatest joys in life lies in resolving the unresolved.

Learning to love in the absence of love. Learning to laugh in the face of sadness, etc. This follows the Law of Duality wherein everything is experienced in relation to its opposite.

It is common for most of us to feel, at some level, that we're not quite good enough or worthy enough to be loved. This is also closely associated with a sense of impending abandonment. These feelings undoubtedly originated early in our childhoods when we did indeed feel abandoned, left out, or incapable in one way or another.

As adults, at some subconscious level we maintain those same childhood expectations of failure and/or abandonment, and bring into play counter-productive coping strategies developed as a child in order to cope with the powerful emotional feelings that accompany those situations.

Coping methods that protected us as children backfire on us as adults.

Hiding our emotions helped us through terrifying moments as children, but as adults the same behavior isolates us from the very love we yearn for and deserve in relationships. It can also lead to non-productive 'people-pleasing,' passive-aggressive backstabbing behavior, a propensity to be late, and intermittent reinforcement routines; all of which rob the good oil from any relationship and usually and ultimately lead to the failure of the relationship.

Alternatively, latent and unexpressed early innocent rage often manifests later in life as an intense sense of victimhood wherein we project that early anger overtly onto those we are actively trying to love.

What is actually happening during these heartbreak scenarios is that our ambiguous childhood coping mechanisms lead us to sabotage our own later relationships. This leads to an inevitable self-fulfilling abandonment caused by a combination of our sense of guilt, the anger coming from our innocent rage, and the internal trauma shock of the new heartbreak impacting directly from and back into the original childhood trauma.

You will feel it in your gut.

You will know just how much you wanted and needed the love that has now gone missing.

And if you continue to grieve for long, you may well put in place the seeds of life threatening disease and illness such as cancer, heart disease, diabetes, mental illness, etc.

What is important is that you recognize why this hurts so much, that it is impacting directly on your old childhood wounds, and that you need to resolve the emotion as quickly as you can in order to avoid serious consequences.

Our heartbreaks open up our unresolved childhood wounds, allowing us to distinguish them in our feelings, and presenting yet another opportunity for healing and resolution.

There is a reason, and a season, for all things.

Seize the moment and all it holds. Feel the pain, and resolve it through the healing balm of love.

Only those who are drowning can be saved.

REMEMBERING

I am but a remembrance,
Of love that's come and gone.
Of things I've tried, and times I've failed,
And things that have gone wrong.

I know I've failed more times than not,
I've often been untrue.
But then I wasn't who I am,
And then you were not you.

We lived then in forgetfulness,
How could we know the truth?
We didn't know we didn't know,
That wisdom lost on youth.

But now I'm waking up, you know,
I'm here now, can't you tell?
So make a joyful noise because,
We've <u>both</u> returned from hell.

Come look into my eyes again,
To gaze beyond the veil.
To see things as they really are,
We must be seen as well.

Welcome back into my life,
It's like we never parted.
And open up your heart again,
Let's finish what we started.

Remember & Resolve the Trauma Memory

If you can somehow return to the foundational childhood memory and experience the horror of it fully and completely, it is possible for you to at least partly resolve the wound with your adult understanding, stop blaming all those involved, and then move on with a clean slate, so to speak.

The first step is to identify the original core childhood experience and 'own' it as belonging to you. Consciously allow yourself to feel the emotion entirely. Sit with your emotion until you can identify where in your body it is manifesting from. In the observation of it an interesting phenomenon can occur. Instead of 'being' the emotion, we must stand apart from it in order to observe it. In observing it, we acknowledge it as our own. In taking ownership over it is likely we will then find access to the foundational experience in which we bought into the story or belief that has been haunting us.

Alternatively, imagine yourself traveling through your blood stream in a micro-submarine right to the source of the emotion. Let your body's innate intuition be your guide. Get out and look around. Shine your light on what you see, the results of the unsettled emotional trauma.

Allow your mind to screen the foundational memory in 3 D upon the background of what you are looking at; an organ in upheaval and dissonance. Quite possibly during this process, you will remember the event at the core of the emotion, complete with the horrible feelings that accompany it.

With your adult understanding, and calling in your own higher self, reframe the memory according to your highest wisdom. Release the anger, blame, and guilt that you have been holding all these years. Instead of embracing your abandonment victimhood, shower both your child self and the other persons involved with compassion and love.

You will experience the power of the emotion beginning to fade away as you step into love, and out of anger. It will never disappear, but it will recede into the background in a way in which you can use it later to your advantage in your relationships with others.

Once done, you will learn how to identify the emotion even as it knocks at your door, as it will always be there, waiting for the right moment to knock. By all means, invite it inside, so to speak; but only as a temporary guest, and not as the master of the house. This is simply your still present wounded child looking for the love it never got; at least not in his/her understanding of the event.

With tenderness and compassion 'hold' your child self in his/her pain, expressing as much love as you can in the process. Almost magically, your former victimhood surrounding the unresolved emotion will at the least slowly transform from a re-experiencing of childhood pain into an experience of expressing and receiving love.

You will 'become' the love rather than the pain. With practice you will automatically feel love for yourself each time the old emotion knocks. That old, outgrown emotion will lose its power over you and become another wonderful gift and/or a new tool in your toolbox of loving.

Stand in your pain, honor your wounds, and love the child within.

If not you, then whom?

A PRAYER

Oh, great spirit, help me to remember that life is a game ~ your almighty game ~ and we are the players.

Help us to play your game with vigor, commitment, and passion, that all may be entertained and uplifted by the spectacle.

Help us to remember that every experience and event in our lives is but another opportunity to rise above our own forgetfulness, and manifest your divine presence through love.

Remind us once again that Love stands as a silent witness, even in the midst of confusion, chaos, and catastrophe.

Help us to accept that chaos and loss are powerful mediums in which divine order can manifest.

Why is it, father, that it is only in these times that we look for, listen for, and remember, love?

Could it be that these times are the portals through which we have special opportunity to rise above our anger, fear, and sense of separation?

Could it be that these are the times when we can most easily rediscover you; and in that experience, discover ourselves?

Thank you, father, for loving me. Thank you for blessing others in my life with love, that I might experience you through them.

Thank you father, for letting me see love even in the heart of disaster, reminding me once again that love is all there is.

Repair the Damage
With Love & Understanding

Another option available, once you realize the power and pain of the emotional feelings you are having-and connect the dots back to your childhood traumas- is to review just what behavior it was by which you have sabotaged the relationship.

Sometimes just by understanding the source of your behavior you can alter it and restore love into the relationship. The worst thing you can do is to continue to blame the other person for simply responding to your own actions and your own abuse in the best way they know how to.

There really is no 'right' or 'wrong.'

All things are the manifestation of a perfect karmic balancing act playing itself out in the moment; a direct result of the choices we have made in the past. New choices bring new results.

Changing our behavior changes our outcomes.

I DON'T HAVE TO BE RIGHT

You do not have to make me right; that's not where I belong.
To truly be in now, there's neither right nor wrong.

To make me right and make you wrong is not my true intention.
I only want to be not wrong, that's all there is to mention.

The moment simply is, and in the now is always neutral.
When I attempt to make you wrong, I'm sure the feeling's mutual.

The moment that I make you wrong, the argument gets longer.
The way you justify your stance is just to make me wronger.

I might have made a hurtful choice, for that I'm truly sad.
But just because I stubbed your toe, it doesn't make me bad.

If I forget and make you wrong please tell me if you will.
I only try to do that because I haven't got it still.

Forgive me - it's so hard to stop a habit held so long,
And help me see how hurtfully it interrupts life's song.

So try and understand that I'm not itching for a fight.
And don't forget that I'm not wrong for trying to be right.

Replace the Loss

If the bridges are well and truly burned, the other option is to simply move on quickly. Find another relationship, cultivate new friends, take on a new hobby, etc. Biologically speaking, you have probably experienced the archetypal loss of partner or loss of territory syndrome actuated in the reptilian brain that sets in place at least a temporary change in metabolism.

If this settles deeply within a pre-existing childhood trauma, and does not get resolved quickly, it can very easily transform into life threatening disease. This is why it is important to resolve the issue one way or the other as quickly as possible. And you will sleep better as a result.

It is my understanding that I can love anyone, provided my ego gives a sufficient sign off. I believe it is true for you, too. And it may be helpful to consider who *you* can love rather than looking for someone who can love you. This changes the energy of the situation dramatically.

The trauma of the heartbreak brings a gift along with a curse. The curse is the gnawing metabolic change that grinds away in your gut. The blessing is the enhanced sense of passion that accompanies the experience. Attach your unconditional love to that passion and take it into the next level of relationship.

If you can't fix the relationship that broke down, take that new level of love into another relationship. Once you focus on expressing your love elsewhere rather than groveling in you victimhood, your gut settles down, you sleep better, and you will feel like a completely new person. Refined, with a whole new level of intensity. Born again even.

You have chosen a difficult and challenging life this time around in order to fast-forward your ascension to the CHRIST CONSCIOUSNESS.

Go with the opportunity. Love lies just beyond every hurdle. Take a running leap and you will experience an incredibly soft landing.

Not only will you enjoy it, but you will gain an entirely new appreciation for yourself.

Above all, keep moving. Your journey has just begun.

TO HEAL A BROKEN HEART

The way to heal a broken heart is just to keep on lovin'
How do I know? It is because I must have had a dozen.
Some hurt because I couldn't love the way I wanted to.
And others hurt because I knew how badly I hurt you.

It's all the same, and so are we, when we begin to see,
There's nothing in between of us, I'm you and you are me.
I'm learning now how precious be the love that passes through,
When you accept the love I give, I know you love me, too.

I'm grateful for the valued time you spent in loving me.
I'll not forget your precious gift; it gave me eyes to see.
I'm sad to see you thus depart to seek another 'me,'
And sorry I am sure you know, for you I could not be.

And if it was my choice, sweetheart, somehow to make you mine,
I'd do whatever it would take to love you one more time.
Healing my own wounded heart more easily said than done,
If you won't let me love again, I'll find another 'one'.

That's not the choice I want to make; there's nothing else to do.
Because our love was special, I will always think of you.
The way to heal a broken heart is just to keep on giving.
And then the pain just goes away, and I can keep on living.

Taming the Mighty Elephant

One need only study the technique of domesticating the mighty elephant in order to understand just what happens in the lives of men, and how childhood traumas can, sometimes tragically, shape our adult lives.

It is largely hopeless to attempt to tame a wild adult African or Indian elephant. They are just too large and powerful. Elephant trainers begin with baby elephants either born in captivity or captured shortly after birth.

Even a baby elephant is relatively powerful. Thus the baby elephant is secured with a reasonably stout chain staked solidly into the ground. The baby elephant will pull and pull upon the chain for some time in an attempt to be free. Ultimately, however, the baby elephant succumbs to its circumstances and submits to its chain.

At this time, the elephant will begin to submit to the encouragement of its trainers, taking on whatever tricks or behavior that is required of it to cope with its circumstances. And even as the elephant continues to grow, it is always chained and staked in the same way, with the same chain that was used as a baby. And even as the elephant becomes strong and mighty, it never again challenges its chain, unless some especially traumatic event triggers it to react without thinking. Only then can it summon up its true power in releasing itself from bondage, and in experiencing freedom.

And so it is with humankind. Often it requires a hugely traumatic event to occur in our lives in order to go beyond our own limiting thought processes in rediscovering our true power and our true self. Otherwise, we likely will remain slaves to the beliefs and belief systems we created as small children before we had access to the world of words and wisdom.

I am here to tell you that you are more powerful than the mightiest of the elephants, and the chains of belief that now hold you are puny in comparison to your own powers; if only you choose to activate them. The intensity accompanying your traumatic event, if properly directed towards love rather than victimhood, can oftentimes save a 'lost' relationship, or help create a new relationship.

There are several important elements involved in staying in love. Each, **if** fully activated, can be successful. And a combination of them all in some degree can also work.

Even to access a minute fraction of your innate powers of loving will empower you to be successful in relationship, especially if you can bring your focused intensity to bear on your commitment to love.

The past serves you well provided you do not allow it to enslave you.

Use the passion and intensity of heartbreak to shatter the chains of false belief systems and to discover your latent and unconquerable strengths.

LIVING WITH INTENSITY

A life without intensity a boring thing it be.
To wake up with a yawn each day does not appeal to me.

For I am here to live my life, whatever should pass by;
To be who I have come to be, whatever the cost, say I.

This life is but a single page, there's only so much space
To tell my story to the world, and meet life face to face.

Express then, now, my deepest hope, by which I write this page,
That hope will lead to action, and give love its proper stage.

To journey to the well of life with tiny cup serves none.
To hold enough for others, too, for me is much more fun.

So stretch yourself and go for it, if I may be so bold,
For you might find, as you grow out, there's more that you can hold.

It has been said that life's a blast; holds much that can be found;
But only shows its face to me when I'm in passion bound.

Bless all your good intentions with the energy to 'be.'
Intensity is that which serves intention, don't you see?

So choose your path as best you can, and give it energy.
You'll move far faster on your path with some intensity.

Spiritual Teachings

Many persons do become the outwards expression of love, rather than its needy recipient, through disciplines and guidance already attributed to the various religious teachings. They achieve this once they understand that they *are* love wanting only to be received, seen and reflected back to itself.

My own conscious journey has been predicated by a Presbyterian Christian upbringing. My journey was then intensified during my experience with the Sideras spiritual commune in British Columbia, Canada, which was testing the teachings of Jesus as revealed in the New Testament of the Bible.

What I have experienced since that time, although hinted at throughout various Bible passages, lies well beyond present orthodox Christian doctrine and dogma. In moving beyond doctrine I have discovered perfection; an understanding of the perfect constructive fabric of the universe and our experience of it.

This is not to say that all is bliss. But rather, that everything is designed to assist and hurry us along on our journey towards bliss. The journey becomes bliss only after we set aside the illusion of our circumstances, the guilt and anger of our childhood traumas, and all the false belief systems we have been indoctrinated into.

Therefore leaving the principles of the doctrine of Christ, let us go on unto perfection...

Hebrews 6, v.1

Occasionally people will achieve oneness and connection with God without being consciously aware of how they do it. Some persons come into life with a well-established predisposition for love, and a profound reluctance to buy into all the false gods thrown at them during childhood.   Perhaps Jesus, Buddha, Krishna, and Mohammed were such ones.

And others, such as Down's syndrome children, are so lacking in memory and/or intellectual capacity that love gets through without having to navigate around the stony reefs of ego and circumstance.

I have been wrecked more than once after running aground upon my own false belief systems; one might say barely escaping with my life.

There are many spiritual disciplines that may help. Attaining the state of Grace as spoken about within Christianity is incredibly empowering, both in the experience and appreciation of self, but also in cementing in loving relationships. This is the enlightenment spoken of by gurus and teachers of many different eastern traditions. This is the 'silence beyond all understanding' spoken about by the early Gnostic Christians. This is the 'raising of the Kundalini' taught in some spiritual schools. It is also the 'gap,' the 'zone' and the place of 'now.'

There are scores of scripture and self-development techniques available pointing to one method or another of how to establish a divine connection with love. It doesn't matter how you get there. It only matters that you do.

A joyful connection with another person can be maintained only if we recognize the permanent connection with our own higher self. We can be in love all the time simply by calling upon the divine love bathing us every moment in the Mind of God.

Once we are able to call in and surrender to this universal stream of love, we then become the conduit through which true relationship with another can begin and grow.

We can then be cause in creating relationships from our own infinite strengths, rather than from a needy place of filling our own emptiness or incompleteness.

Our divine mind is always there in the shadows waiting to manifest and express into our lives, provided we simply honor it above the insistent mindless chatter of our own ego and circumstances.

The universe dances – and expands in its experience of itself - when the mind rests.

TO BE OR NOT TO BE

If we should choose not to be,
Then any belief will do.
We can go left, we can go right,
Any place not true.

What have our beliefs obtained for us
But grief and pain and sorrow?
It's not beliefs, but hope that makes
Us rise to greet the morrow.

Our beliefs, you see, can't be in now,
They only know the past.
They keep us firmly anchored there,
To old ideas held fast.

So loose your anchor from what's gone,
And journey into now.
Your beliefs give way to clarity,
Be seen and take a bow!

And lead all others to this place,
Where love and joy stand tall.
The magic place in Eden where
We lived before the fall.

Now even in the beliefs of man,
No matter what they are,
If we proceed with inward faith,
We still might journey far.

God lives within us each, you know,
No matter what his name,
And once you do accept that fact,
You'll never be the same.

The Christ child lives within us all,
Just waiting for the chance,
To rise above our silly beliefs,
To love, to sing, to dance.

It's here, you know, around us still,
You'd see it if you listened.
So join me in this special place,
Just ask and you'll be Christened.

Resting in the Mind of God

I now access this space of oneness by listening to the seven sacred vibrations of creation found within my silence. Years after the British Columbia government reneged on our commune's land purchase deal following the Jonestown suicide massacre in 1971, and forced us to abandon and vacate the property after spending perhaps a million dollars developing roads and bridges, I continued to meditate after the ringing I had first discovered at the commune.

Around 1995 I noticed during a particularly deep meditation that my ringing was coming precisely from the left side of my head. This lead to some curiosity, and a deeper 'listening.' Surprisingly I found another higher ringing on the right side. Within days I was experiencing four or five ringings simultaneously, always leading to a deeper and more profound experience of myself and all my sensory perceptions.

This state of being also made me at least temporarily more connectable and loveable in my relationships with others. As a result of these higher ringings, my spiritual journey accelerated. I enjoyed several amazing, both short-lived and long term relationship experiences, wrote several books of limited success, and then, just as my spiritual life was taking off, I ran smack dab into a legal battle over intellectual property that seemed to flatten me as effectively as if I had just run into a brick wall.

Not only did I lose my way; I lost my marriage, my business, my factory, my home, my money and a large part of my self-esteem. And all my family relationships were thrown into chaos.

Consequently, it took me ten years to fend off the illegitimate patent infringement claims that had been leveled against me. In 2006, the New Zealand Supreme Court ruled in my favor on the major issue, and in late 2009 I finally succeeded against the latent minor claims that had not previously been resolved.

At that time I went on the offensive in a legal sense, and now have several cases before the courts: one a damages claim for groundless threats of patent infringement, one for many years of copyright infringement against my own designs, and one for the revocation of the proven invalid patent at the basis of the original trials.

I have litigated in my own interest since 2006, and have at least been successful enough to navigate these cases through a dozen court appearances to date. This has restored my confidence in myself and allowed me to return more energetically to my original spiritual journey.

Around late August of 2010, while meditating deeply to my ringings, I experienced a convergence of seven distinct vibrations in my mind. When the seven merged I felt myself being inundated with the divine energy of unconditional love. I realized that the ringings were the vibrations of unconditional love which I had been feeling subconsciously in my mind, and in my heart, all along.

This ecstatic experience led me to drop to my knees in gratitude to be the recipient of such love. Truly it was life-changing.

I merged with the ONE MIND in this experience, a universal mind that was composed entirely of unconditional love. I felt that in some way the ONE MIND was experiencing its own completion and fulfillment through my connection with the seven ringings. We *were* the ONE MIND.

Shortly afterwards, I went online and Googled: 'Do you hear the ringings?' What emerged were around 15 million hits on what type of drug or treatment was most effective in making tinnitus (ringing in the ears) go away. Apparently, fully ten percent of the adult population experiences these ringings sooner or later. And most people expend considerable energy in trying to escape from them.

I was incredulous at the almost universal stupidity of trying to make my 'voice of God' go away.

Finally, I came upon a blog that pointed me to Madam Blavatsky, the co-founder of the Theosophical Society. Madam Blavatsky was a controversial figure in her day, claiming numerous spiritual qualities and abilities that were never entirely proved or disproved. In the last year of her life she wrote The Secret Doctrine to explain her philosophy. She reveals her experience and belief that, in order to find God, the pilgrim must 'slay the seven mystic sounds.'

She then went on to describe the various qualities of ringing that she experienced:

> 'Before thou set'st thy foot upon the ladder's upper rung, the ladder of the mystic sounds, thou hast to hear the voice of thy inner GOD in seven manners.
> The first is like the nightingale's sweet voice chanting a song of parting to its mate.
> The second comes as the sound of a silver cymbal of the Dhyanis, awakening the twinkling stars.
> The next is as the plaint melodious of the ocean-sprite imprisoned in its shell.
> And this is followed by the chant of Vina.
> The fifth like sound of bamboo-flute shrills in thine ear.
> It changes next into a trumpet-blast.
> The last vibrates like the dull rumbling of a thunder-cloud.
> The seventh swallows all the other sounds. They die, and then are heard no more.
> When the six are slain and at the Master's feet are laid, then is the pupil merged into the ONE, becomes that ONE and lives therein.'

Blavatsky's description of the ringings closely follows my own experience and is expressed in similar terms. I was struck by the apparent fact that not only were these ringings practical and predictable, they were also imminently teachable. I realized that this was something that I would one day be teaching to others.

I experience these vibrations as various qualities of ringing, white noise similar to the old TVs after transmitting was shut down, a 'whoosh' of energy, internal chimes, subtle bells, the clicking sound of crickets or cicadas, the sound of the sea in a conch shell, and sometimes even an intermittent piercing ringing that merges with the others once I begin, once again, to pay attention.

The ringings become profoundly life changing only when I listen for the feelings that accompany them. The moment that I listen for the feeling in the 'song' my heart opens even more.

In that space of the seven ringings I *become* the vibrations of creation experienced through this human manifestation. It is an experience beyond words, and one that leaves me in the throes of infinite and eternal gratitude. Gratitude for the very gift of being alive and conscious within this amazingly beautiful, magical, and wonderful playground we call life. I merge with and become one with the ONE MIND of God.

I become the silence, listening to and feeling the manifestations of my own vibrations.

It may be that you will experience this space through another door. Perhaps some will 'follow the light' and find god within, just as many persons have followed the light towards God while having a near death experience. By looking into the darkness with your inner vision, darkness reveals itself as dancing light pixels emitting directly from out the soul of God.

Others will 'see the light' as it emits and reflects from another's eyes. In my understanding, this is becoming one with the ONE SOUL of God. Be the source, looking out upon the manifestations and reflections of your own divine light. Feel the vibration of light as it communicates with your heart.

Others will first 'feel' the vibrations as they pass outwardly through the heart. Loving from the heart does not require Tantric intimacy. But it does invoke connection with the ONE HEART of the Christ Consciousness. Be the emptiness, feeling the vibration of love passing in and out through your one shared heart, even at a distance.

If you are a 'feeler' it may be helpful to you to distinguish an audible quality to your love feelings, thereby creating yet another pathway towards God.

Grace, in all its manifestations, does not belong exclusively to any particular religion or discipline. In fact, the adherence to any particular religious or spiritual doctrine can place an almost insurmountable barricade between man and his divine essence.

One practical beauty of following the silence through the seven sacred sounds is that the various vibrations create a type of road map that I can follow in an almost linear manner through the different levels. Undoubtedly, this is the experience described in the account of 'Jacob's ladder' in the Old Testament of the Bible.

When I fully embrace even the lower multiple ringings, the vibrations then express inwardly and outwardly through my soul, eyes, and heart as well. In fact, even to begin to intentionally experience the inner ringings opens me to wonderful connective experiences with the outer world. And that lends itself as a wonderful incentive to learn, experience, and *become* even more. Meditation by any means is empty and meaningless unless it reaches the point of bringing joy to the participant. If there's no joy, I'm simply not looking, listening, or feeling in the right place or at the right frequency at that particular time.

Many people hear the ringing and make nothing of it, save as a nuisance. The important key for me was when I began to feel them in my heart as well. This is when I discovered the ringings as the voice, and song, of love.

As I write this book it is nearly three years since my first experience in the seven ringings. It is 25 March 2013. In the last week, I have broken the last chains from my unresolved childhood abandonment trauma and find myself permanently and truly walking in the mind and love of God.

I have found comfort.

There are no chains of bondage that hold so fast as those we forged with our own mind. Keys to unlocking the mind lie both within it and above it.

Who hath ears to hear, let him hear.

Matthew 13, v.9

The Power of Listening

In my experience the best listeners also happen to be the wisest and happiest persons I know. Is this mere coincidence, or an indication that there is a profound link between listening, wisdom, and happiness?

For my part, I believe that listening is the very key to wisdom and happiness; the very touchstone of unconditional love, and loving. Is it not true that we all love to be truly seen and heard? And that those persons we love the most are those who give themselves most completely in hearing and seeing how it really is for us?

How rare it is to find someone who has both the time and inclination to hear us out in all of our fears, anguish, disappointments, frustrations, dreams, successes, and conquests? Now that is a true friend, indeed.

Deep listening is a learned skill that can be easily acquired. It is all the more easily learned once we know what is at stake, and what the payoff might be.

It has taken me many years to fully comprehend what lies at the foundation of deep listening; and during all that time I wasn't pursuing the art with anything close to a passion or discipline. In the end I came upon it almost by accident, simply by following the gentle ringing in my mind that seemed at first to be merely an interesting curiosity.

That curiosity has now become the basic vehicle of my self-expression. It is an enigma all to itself, as the very act of listening deeply empowers me to be a conduit through which universal love expresses outwardly through me.

My inescapable conclusion is this: as we listen, we love. And the more deeply we listen, the more deeply we love. And the more deeply we listen, the more deeply we, ourselves, experience love in the expression of it.

You don't have to be a trained priest, psychologist, or social worker to benefit from deep listening. And the fact is, even persons in those professions rarely discover the real payoff, because they are taught within their discipline to empathize with rather than to embrace; to ensure that they are not personally caught up in/with what they are hearing and seeing.

This is shallow listening at best, underlining the limitations inherent in even the most well-meaning of our professions. In listening deeply and unconditionally, each of us can do and be what few, if any of our professional 'healers' are able to do; even with their vast array of learned expertise, chemicals, surgical interventions, and drugs.

The first beneficiary is ourselves.

Only when we are able to 'hear' and express the divine essence of love from within ourselves are we able to be real and true lovers to those around us in our lives. Only when we are able to listen truly and deeply to our own higher selves are we then able to express that 'listening' to those around us; allowing them to begin to experience real love, perhaps for the first time in their lives.

That is our most important mission in this life and our greatest opportunity.

There is a grand order to the universe. We are as much a part of it as it is of us. Our very existence proves its merit and sustainability. Science is continually creating new phrases and theories in an attempt to define and understand what existence is. We have string theory, chaos theory, big bang theory, theory of relativity, and a host of others; all attempting to reduce the infinite to fit into the finite.

And at the foundation of modern scientific thinking, always, there must remain the symbol of light.

The fact is, it's *all* light and it's all in constant movement. Always expressing itself. To us, and to whoever, or whatever, is watching and listening. Science calls it electromagnetism, gravity, and light. And at the leading edge of science is the understanding that there is an as yet indefinable energy inherent in everything that defies our attempts to measure or replicate it.

Whether or not science accepts that energy as being real, Science knows that everything affects everything else. So we, too, are part of a grand holistic energy system that is always expressing, and always being expressed upon.

We, as human beings, have the amazing ability to give meaning to those expressions, and to interpret them in a way that fulfills not only our own lives, but the entire cosmos.

Even inanimate objects express to us. In the simplest terms, 'things' express color, shape, texture, smell, taste and form. They also express, through the so called electromagnetic nature of things, a more subtle message not so easily perceived. There is a body of scientific work that supports the notion that even inanimate things change or alter their nature when they are seen and/or perceived.

In other words, when we 'listen' deeply to our environment with all our senses, it may well be that our environment speaks back to us with more and deeper information about what it is, and what we are.

There is a mountain of evidence regarding animate things; those things holding some sort of life force within. Plants, insects, animals and humans; we all respond in some way to being truly seen for what we are. This is particularly apparent in dogs and cats, and with small children. All are vying for our attention in the hope that we will validate their existence. They're all looking for love, just like you and I.

Unfortunately, the modern paradigm has us, almost without exception, looking outside of ourselves for love. So many lives wasted and lost, searching and waiting for someone else to give them love.

The irony is that each of us holds within the means to acquire and express infinite and unconditional love from within. We are all human tuning forks designed to resonate with and receive the divine love that is constantly being broadcast, held and being held by the creative source of the universe.

All we need do is to tune in to the divine frequencies which reside within our own silence, patiently waiting to be heard and applied to our own very significant life.

This is where and when the magic really begins. Because, once we learn to listen to and receive the love that is constantly being gifted towards us, we then become expressions of that same energy. Our deep listening then becomes a divine outward expression of love that blesses all things and all people within our practical energy field, and beyond.

The world then begins to speak into our listening, begins to feel itself/ themselves being heard for the perfect entity(s) that they are, and begins to express itself/themselves back to us as the divine love that it/they have always, in forgetfulness, been. And that is when we begin to experience ourselves as a part of the God that is, looking back upon itself in another human face. This is an almost unspeakably beautiful experience that, in a single moment, justifies the entire universe.

Look, and you shall be seen.

Listen, and you shall be heard.

Feel, and you shall be known.

It is our human-ness that defines our being.

It is also our human-ness that endears us to others.

OUR TRINITY

Our life begins alone and senseless,
As we feel a 'new born' denseness.
Then towards partnership we grow,
Till balanced nature, we then know.

The physical and spirit merging,
Soul and ego, too, converging,
Feeling whole within our skin,
Before we let another in.

To trust ourselves is prerequisite,
Before another's trust we visit,
To trust another's said intent
And trust we know just what they meant.

We risk the danger hidden there
That they, their promise, cannot bear,
Or, we misunderstood their aim.
If so we've only self to blame.

We must be clear in words we say,
And 'be our word' from day to day.
In love that is the only way,
Or love in partnership won't stay.

Together we choose dreams to make.
Together we anticipate
Completion in the path we walk;
A path we've built from out our talk.

Completion comes with these conditions.
It's just the same in all renditions.
When with another we dare go
To be in love and make it so.

We're not alone within this game.
Another, too, seeks just the same,
And helps when two choose to be three,
You, Me and Love, our Trinity.

Relationship.
Why is it so Difficult to 'Get it?'

Pure information always exists. We are constantly being bombarded by the seven vibrations of creation which manifest both our reality and our illusion. Both are inherently dependent upon each other as the dual basis for experience and completion. However, we are who we are, whatever we pretend to be, or pretend *not* to be.

One man can be experiencing the bliss of 'Heaven,' while another standing alongside can be experiencing the torments of 'Hell.' How can this be?

Our thoughts of the past or the future are actually snapshots out of time. We can connect with those other times in order to gain understanding and foresight, or in order to gift our love to those who were/will be in need; but we can only truly 'be' in the sacred now of our present incarnation.

The very moment we pretend to be other than the divine entity we are or where we are; or, we attempt to define this moment by comparing it to a past moment; an interesting phenomenon occurs. We lose access to the pure information/energy/vibration – call it what you will - that exists around us in this moment. This 'present' information doesn't get through to us.

We are left to experience that which was; or who we thought ourselves to be. Most often, this 'pretend' person is wrought with self-judgments, past criticisms, memories of past failures and the pain of past punishments. Any information entering the mind in the present is filtered through these layers of the past; the mind looking for information that fits the preconceived notion of who, or what, the person perceives him/herself to be. In other words, we 'hear' only what we 'listen for. The other stuff doesn't get through. We don't hear it, so we can't process it.

The information/reality of paradise does not disappear; it is not visible or audible to us because it has been covered over by our own thoughts, beliefs, and judgments. This is sometimes called cognitive dissonance. Does God take Paradise away from us? Hardly. We disappear from Paradise.

Why would anyone step out of Paradise?

No one chooses to be unhappy. No one chooses to feel hurt, time after time. No one chooses to feel rejected, unloved, frustrated, angry or invalidated. There is a simple physiological process by which we unknowingly sabotage and invalidate ourselves.

I believe that we are beings of pure energy, resonating with the vibrations of our choice, depending entirely upon our present level of spiritual development and understanding. The energy that we experience follows the electromagnetic pattern, or frequency, of our choice. All of our senses are electromagnetic receivers and generators, especially our minds and our hearts. We are human tuning forks of divine energy. When we tune in, we come alive. When we come alive, we broadcast; carrying the tone of who we are like a tuning fork.

These energy fields, whether vibrational or electromagnetic, interact with, and affect each other. With magnets, and in all electromagnetic systems, positive repels positive and negative repels negative. Likewise the positive expression of love connects with someone or something open to receive it. And our willingness to receive love creates the space within which another person can express into. However, the moment we turn our minds or hearts 'on' to retrieve from the past, we create a sort of electromagnetic field around us which prevents real information –and love- from the present entering or leaving.

We cannot realistically be in two places at the same time, in two times at the same time, or in two opposite vibrations at the same time. At least until after we master the art of being totally present in one time or place. Likewise, when we tune into our thoughts, it's impossible to simultaneously tune into and experience the divine love/information that is always 'speaking' to us through our hearts. Our thoughts can define a particular question relevant in the moment, but the answer must come from within the moment itself.

The very moment we begin to 'think' we lose access to our true being in the present. The very moment we begin to interpret, to judge, to decide, to compare, to worry, or to fear, we lose access to the wonderful energy/information about ourselves that is washing over us each moment.

We create an electromagnetic thought barrier through which nothing real can penetrate. We vibrate at a frequency of non-being; a frequency of illusion and imagination.

Which of you by taking thought can add one cubit unto his stature?

Matthew 6, v.27

There are times when you can actually recognize this is happening with another person.

Have you ever met someone new and had a sense that at some point in the conversation, they seemed to retract physically from you? As if they actually took two steps back, but didn't actually do it. If you were looking into their eyes at that moment, you might have seen the pupils contract to tiny peepholes, limiting the amount of light and information from coming in or going out. The electromagnetic filter has gone up! They have gone somewhere else.

Or sometime else.

You needn't know where. It might be slightly uncomfortable going there, even if you could. But it is very helpful to know when this other person has left you, because there's nothing else you can say about 'what is' or about 'who you are' that will be heard. You might as well pack your bags and be on your way.

Maybe they've just come to realize 'who you were.' That you were a competitor at some level. Maybe you were a perceived enemy or threat to them or to their friends. Maybe they've heard some unsavory gossip about you, and think they already know you. Maybe you'd just said something that threatened one of their closely held belief systems.

Or maybe they were projecting some part of their past onto you; expecting you to fulfill some negative expectation built upon *their* past experience; reliving through you, an uncomfortable dynamics experienced early in life with a principal caregiver.

And maybe they decided, for one reason or another out of their own past, that you just don't measure up to their own peculiar belief system.

The moment another person thinks they know you they lose access to who you really are; and to who *they* are.

The moment a person thinks they know themselves, they lose access to themselves; and *you* lose access to them, as well.

The 'thinking mechanism' may be responsible, not only for countless failed relationships, but for many of our physical diseases, as well. It may well be that all, or most, disease occurs as a result of emotional energy at an electromagnetic level being captured or held by the electromagnetic or auric fields of the various organs or bodily systems.

As an energy being immersed in an electromagnetic and/or vibratory energy field, our greatest and most profound experiences of life occur when we are open and in permission to the continuing flow of energy through our body; energy coming from, vibrating with, and reflecting back to the Quantum Hologram, the name given by science to the 'standing wave' nature of the cosmos.

Whenever we dwell on the past, our electromagnetic or vibratory frequency changes, preventing healing and life-giving energy from working through us. We experience fears, phobias, anger, grief and other 'energy blockages,' which can then manifest as physical illnesses within our bodies. When we think upon these emotions, giving them more and more negative energy, the expression of them is unable to be released through the electromagnetic or vibratory frequency of the 'now.'

This energy is then forced to settle somewhere in the physical or auric body; giving rise to a host of possible diseases.

These blockages can sometimes be cleared with different types of body work including massage, qi gong, reiki, acupuncture, t'ai chi, or any of a host of disciplines developed for this very purpose.

There are numerous electromagnetic balancing devices which seem able to 'burn away' disease causing emotional blockages, as well. One such machine created by Royal Rife nearly 80 years ago is still widely used for this purpose. I have had a positive personal experience with a machine called the Quantum Booster, an electromagnetic device developed for the treatment of cancers and other diseases, which also seems helpful towards developing meditation skills and in settling sufferers of ADD (Attention Deficit Disorder.)

And the medical profession continues to use electric or electromagnetic shock treatment to lift patients at least temporarily from the grip of chronic depression.

Recent discoveries in biochemistry point to the emerging importance of newly discovered glyconutrients, and other subtle food nutrients that now appear to be hugely important in the transfer of information from cell to cell. The entire body immune system is based upon the flow of energy and information, between cells. Evidence is emerging that all allergy and disease, even from a genetic nature, may be caused by a failed transfer of pure energy, memory, and information between cells.

Anything that enhances this transfer serves health, and life. However, the best food and the best medical treatments are all relatively powerless against significant unresolved childhood trauma experiences.

When we are lost within our circumstances – whether past or present- proper nutrition, exercise, and lifestyle will help in preserving our opportunity to grow into our larger spiritual selves. As we become more consciously aware, our choices in these areas become much more simple and obvious, even as their significance wanes.

Once we begin to access the pure energy of being (prana) our bodies become more efficient and relatively independent from an energy point of view. It then becomes less important to follow a strict lifestyle regime; provided our mental and spiritual regime remains sound and intact.

We lived for days on nothing but food and water.

W. C. Fields

The mind, the imagination and the memory can be more dangerous and self-destructive than dynamite, when handled and used without respect and understanding.

The mind is the domain of the past, the place where fear and all negative emotions originate. To be afraid requires us to retrieve some negative experience from the past and superimpose a similar expectation upon the present. The present then 'becomes' the past, and the worst of the past at that. To live in fear destroys our access to the present; the place where love lives.

All our emotional hang-ups are predicated upon a faulty and/or unbalanced thought process. We create a story in our mind based upon incomplete information, and then mentally chain ourselves to the story unless or until we are able to rewrite it with new and more accurate information.

By linking our thought process to the Divine Mind we can un-think our childhood traumas by illuminating them with the light of love. Like a thief, the past has little power in the light of the eternal now, which is love.

The mind can behave like a destructive and unruly child, but when disciplined can support us like a trusted servant.

Like weeding a garden, abandoning unhelpful judgments from our past allows light and truth to shine upon our relationships.

He that feareth is not made perfect in Love.

I John 4, v.18

YOU'RE NOT WHO YOU PRETEND TO BE

You're not who you pretend to be, it really doesn't matter.
You can't escape your destiny, not even if you're badder.

You see, the now is all there is, we can't escape the moment.
No matter where we hide inside, it only causes torment.

The past is gone, it matters not what we have done or said.
The past is not alive no more; it may as well be dead.

Our ghosts are those that we still choose, the masks we wear each day.
The judgments that we hide behind like children at their play.

So take them off and free yourself for more of life's true bliss.
The longer that we hide from self, the more of life we miss.

A part of you is here with me just waiting for the chance
To join in perfect harmony the rhythm of life's dance.

So come outside and play with me stripped naked of the past,
And run beneath the hose of life through rainbows thick and fast.

We're really meant to play at life, it all is just a game.
To think that God has made mistakes is really quite insane.

Remember this throughout your game it's not to win or lose.
To love or hate, this is our choice - we get just what we choose.

Observing the Seven Vibrations

The first ringing: '*I* am not alone.'
When I first began to hear the ringing, I was filled with an incomparable feeling of no longer being alone. To know that there was some other 'thing' connecting me to a higher source gave me new hope, and a new strength to carry on against the considerable adversity occurring within my personal, social, and business life at the time.

You may experience this sense of not being alone in your own unique way without the ringings. However, it may be helpful for you to try to distinguish an audio quality to any not-alone feelings. To hear and distinguish the first ringing is the most daunting step towards mastery of the seven mystic sounds or vibrations of creation.

The second ringing: '*We* are not alone.'
Discovering the second ringing years later opened an entirely new dimension of possibilities to me. Were there more, higher vibrations? What did they mean? Immediately I noticed a profound change in the way I began relating with and to others.

The second ringing seemed to cement in and bring closer the concept of human relationship within the fold of my own connection to the other, higher self. In a sense this created a kind of triangular blueprint mirroring the scriptural Holy Trinity, wherein any two persons bringing their own higher selves to relationship then invoke a new higher connective energy, or synergy, with the divine.

This is when I actively began pursuing more meaningful relationships; and stepping away from those that seemed stagnant, used up and/or non-receptive. The higher ringings are not required in order to begin to connect with others in a deeper spiritual manner.

The possibility of a new and deeper relationship with another person answered one question and raised another. 'Was I lovable?'

For where two or three are gathered together in my name, there am I in the midst of them.

Matthew 18, v.20

The third ringing: 'I *am* lovable.'

My twenty-five year marriage ended, and in its place new magic began to happen. My first relationship after that marriage break-up brought with it an amazing new experience of being loved beyond anything that I had experienced for years.

Barbara was definitely one of the loves of my life; gifting to me a fresh new realization that I could be loved – and loved more deeply - in spite of myself. And with that experience came a wonderful merging of our physical bodies wherein we became, for a short while, the **ONE BODY** of Christ. This was an expression of Tantric connection or 'Oneness' that is widely spoken about within the Hindu culture.

We became the **ONE BODY**, and at least temporarily shared aspects of the **ONE SOUL** that I had previously experienced in reflection with Angus Cherrington many years before, and the **ONE MIND** experience that I access through my own inner ringings. And thus, the third ringing seems to be related to the vibration of lovability; a very important milestone in my, and anyone's spiritual journey of destiny. You do not have to hear the third ringing in order to feel lovable. But if you do, you surely will feel lovable.

Accepting that you are lovable opens many new doors of possibility. Should you connect with someone who understands the magic of loving, you will be transformed in the experience of being loved; and very likely springboard towards a new experience of being cause in the expression of loving.

101

On the other hand, accepting yourself as being lovable, and experiencing that in a relationship, does not cement it in as an on-going lifetime experience unless you also move up the vibrational level to become the expression of love as well as its destination.

My relationship with Barbara failed because I had not yet realized my role in being the outward expression of love. When she found it hard to love me (I can be difficult at times) I had no idea of why or how I could continue to love her.

The fourth ringing: 'I love.'
The fourth ringing, or rung on the ladder of spiritual growth, brought to me a clear new realization that the juice of life and loving lies in the outward expression of that love. It is one thing to be temporarily loved, and many persons experience that during a 'common' lifetime.

But sooner or later, in the absence of a deeper understanding and expression of love in an outward manner, being loved more often than not leads to the eventual loss of that love due to neglect, ignorance, or a lack of reciprocity on the part of one party or another. The fourth ringing reveals the magic of loving outwardly, which is not necessarily a thing of actively doing; but rather of actively 'being.' Love expresses as a pure vibration, as well as through speech, action, and prayer.

Some persons love easily; perhaps even too easily, without realizing the importance of finding someone who is capable of truly receiving the gifts they bring. This often results in a 'broken heart.' Painful as it was for me to experience, my broken heart on occasion has forced me to go deeper into my true feelings, allowed me to let in a little more light upon the situation, and has given me a real opportunity to try out new untried spiritual gifts of unconditional loving. Dealing with my broken heart raised some very important questions about what and who I was, and from where the pain really came.

Ultimately I discovered my childhood abandonment issue was at the core of my broken heart and, with considerable thoughtful attention, I at least partially resolved it. This experience allowed more of my untapped inner love to escape outwardly to bless my outer universe, and even perhaps blessed me with my first real experience of learning to love myself unconditionally. Only when I learned to love simply for the sake of loving- for the wonderful feeling of love expressing outwardly from my heart- did I begin to understand the meaning of unconditional love.

The fullness of this experience in the fourth ringing arrived only after I began to listen for the *feeling* of this vibration ringing in and out through my heart.

The fifth ringing: 'I am.'

The expression of love as active 'being-ness' emits naturally from the fifth ringing. The 'I am' realization offers a sense of completeness within oneself. I can love and am worthy to be loved. In fact I stand within love completely and entirely whenever I let go of my outer circumstances and remember that I am complete within myself, and that love is constantly flowing through my heart.

The fifth ringing became my natural foundation after finally resolving major karmic lessons from my past lives. This is not necessarily a state of bliss, but rather a solid state of being comfortable in my skin whatever is going on around me. The bliss comes in whenever there is a permissive opportunity to love another person, or when my life affords me the time and pleasure to ascend higher to the sixth or seventh vibrations.

The sixth ringing: 'I am love.'

The sixth ringing reveals the truth about who and what I really am. I am no longer a physical being having a spiritual experience, i.e., experiencing God's love; I realize and understand that I am love itself expressing myself through this humble earthly manifestation that calls itself Carl Peterson. This heralds in the experience of passively loving my pure state of being.

The seventh ringing: 'I am God.'
The seventh ringing merges me with myself. Being love manifest, I become a part of God manifest. I understand that all things are created by, and held within my word, which *is* love. That all things are perfectly manifested by my word and by my thought; and that every experience that I have had in this or past lives has come about by my own choice, my own intention, and by my own divine design.

Without all the karmic lessons chosen by myself, including many lifetimes of suffering and pain, I would never have learned the truth about myself, and would never have been able to experience my own Godhood as it is opening up for me now as I write this book.

More than anything else, the seventh ringing is about bliss. The pure bliss of vibrating to the tune of love as only the divine master can play. This is resting blissfully within the mind, body and soul of God.

We are all Gods.
There are many pathways towards God. No one needs to hear the ringings as I have in order to experience their own Godhood. Finding our karmic destiny as a manifestation of God is as much about letting go of all that which is not of God as it is grabbing on to some aspect of what God is.

In becoming Love, we naturally release our grip from upon what is not love; and it releases its grip from upon us. So, when we release our grip from upon what is not love, we naturally move closer to the love that we are and have always been at our core. When thought ceases, God speaks into our silence. When we listen, we feel love.

There is a seventh heaven, and you already own a mansion
there. But what is the use of it if you insist on living elsewhere?

*...Is it not written in your law, I said, Ye are
gods?*

John 10, v.34

WHO AM I?

I am the great eternal flame of God, burning within a single soul.
I am the selfless warrior, giving myself up for the life cause.
I am the victim, experiencing a place from which remembering can begin, and pain, end.
I am the victor, in each new remembering finding respite from darkness and death.
I am the precious metal in the boiling cauldron, being purified in the fire of truth.
I am the cauldron of self knowledge, holding within me all that I was, all that I am, and all that I may be.
I burn like the fire from which I come, a friend and lover uncompromising in truth and honesty.
I am that pure energy of love that the world dare not look upon, lest it be purged of its treachery and self denial.
Look not too deeply into my eyes unless you, too, be ready to journey on in truth; naked, and consumed by fire.
I know you, even if you know me not.
Know me, if you truly wish to know yourself.
I am the eternal flame of God, burning within <u>this</u> single soul, naked and on fire.
I am the fire from which I come. I am your fire, and you, mine.
Burn me with your passion, in anger and hurt, as well as joy.
Who are you, that you know not I, or yourself?
I am the eternal flame of God, burning within a single soul.

Connecting Through the Heart of God

Some of us have a greater predisposition for experiencing the vibrations of creation through their tactile or 'feeling' senses. When two people exchange the exquisite sensation of touch in intimate relationship, an experience can occur wherein the two separate bodies truly become the **ONE BODY** expressing the **HEART OF GOD**.

The sensitivity and experience of the participants is entirely dependent upon the depth and frequency of the vibrations they are sharing. This type of spiritual connection with the divine essence is commonly called Tantric sexuality.

Any experience of touching another person is a journey towards the Heart of God. Any experience that deepens one's feeling and appreciation of the physical senses contributes to that journey.

Many persons begin to feel connection to the Heart of God while lost in physical dance, listening to or playing music, singing, practicing t'ai chi, yoga or other body disciplines, or simply when becoming deeply aware of one's own breathing during meditation. All roads lead to home.

Experiencing solely through the heart vibrations does not offer the same sort of instructive road map towards the divine experience as does the inner ringings, because it is difficult to gauge the frequency or magnitude of the vibrations present. In one sense you're either there or you're not.

But in the end, it's all about feelings, whether they arrive through sight, hearing, or touch.

Those only hearing the ringings should strive to attach a feeling quality to them in order to deepen the experience.

Those only feeling the vibrations will benefit by also attaching an audio quality to them. This then becomes an alternate avenue of entry.

Surrendering to the body in this way may very well open up channels into both the mind of God and through the eyes (soul) of God.

Mind, body, soul. The one God experienced in whole or part.

ODE TO BARBARA

There are but two things hard in life we do alone.
From past forgotten we emerge alone at birth.
So, too, in death we leave our loves of life and venture on alone.

But from our birth we strive to join again with life
Through all things seen and felt,
One day to seek and find our own reflection
Mirrored in the calming waters of another's soul.

We do not come alive to stand alone and gaze back at the universe.
The rose when cut blooms once then wilts,
No roots to nourish and sustain.

If we should love but once and carry sorrow all our life,
With eyes downcast pass by and miss perhaps the love that comes again.

We grow through nourishment in love not once but every time we seek.
We gain not love from any but they give themselves to love,
As we in perfect symmetry.

We cannot choose to love and whom,
For love might choose to smile not on us.
How better still to love ourself and offer self to those in need.
Perhaps our cup by portions shall be filled for all eternity.

Pity those who find in love a moment of infinity,
And seek forever more the end and not the means,
Like foolish drunkards numbed to life
And well beyond enchantment by the brew.

Connecting Through the Soul of God

It has been said that the eyes are the windows of the soul. And how true that is. Eye contact is by far the most important way we connect and communicate with one another. The eyes catch much that words miss; and at the higher levels of being, the eyes can convey an entire language in an energy of their own.

I can identify several different levels of clairvoyance in relationship, each of which differs remarkably from the normal human experience wherein strangers rarely make comfortable eye contact with one another. In fact, many cultures forbid such eye contact, seriously eroding the true wealth and value of that culture.

Once we become familiar and comfortable with friends and family members, we let our boundaries drop a little and often make comfortable eye contact during conversation as a subtle way to acknowledge and express love and friendship. This is akin to relating in the first and second vibrations wherein relationship becomes an important marker on our spiritual journey. Though it's relatively commonplace it is certainly not the norm, and for even this level of connection to occur there must be a significant element of earned trust present in the relationship.

More rarely I have made eye contact with someone I have just met and been shocked by the radiant beauty I see in their eyes. And I know that they are seeing the same beauty in my own eyes. I am moved in my heart in this experience, and rejoice at the feeling of love that accompanies it. In sharing this, I have likely invoked at least the fourth ringing and they the third, temporarily accepting their own lovability within my expression of love. It may even be the other way around. We both must be cause in the experience.

At this level of connection, the experience is deeply satisfying; quickly demarcating the distinction between casual friendships and real soul mates. However, unless there is some basis for trust in the reflection, this is most likely to be a brief and perhaps one-off experience; unless, of course, both persons involved have actually learned to begin trusting in themselves and are actively seeking out this level of connection with others. At the present time a relatively few persons have achieved the means to communicate regularly at this level of connection.

Even more rarely, perhaps only a handful of times in my post-commune experience, the love I see in another person's eyes radiates back at me as circular orbs of exquisite magical energy dancing back and forth between we two participants totally embracing our hearts as well as our eyes. At this level the eyes are subservient to the heart. Beautiful as the eyes be, it is the heart that calls for connection. A connection at this level demands renewal and continuation. No one can easily walk away. For this connection to occur, we both must be participating at the level of the fourth and fifth vibrations of creation. Few are they to behold such a beautiful view of the great soul, precious beyond words; and impossible to experience by a lone traveler.

While I lived in the British Columbia commune in the early 70s, many people were experiencing this level of communication around me, without actually accessing beyond the first 'audio' ringing. Undoubtedly, we had been accessing the higher vibrations via the ONE SOUL of Christ rather than the ONE MIND of Christ.

My experience in the British Columbia commune with Angus Cherrington was the ultimate in clairvoyance wherein we blessed each other with the opportunity to see right into the ONE SOUL of Christ which was the very universe itself. This was looking with the eyes, feeling with the heart, and understanding with the mind; right into the very soul of GOD. Without doubt, this was looking through the seventh vibration of creation, just as Krishna's mother did long ago.

My previous beliefs defined a timid and imperfect universe. How wrong could I be?

*Thou shalt love the Lord thy God with all thy
heart, and with all thy soul, and with all thy
mind.*

Matthew 22, v.37

IN LOVE WITH LOVE

*I stand in love like a bitch on heat. Accepting all overtures.
Allowing love to use me as it will.*

*I create no expectations, nor allow any to move me from my high and holy
silence in Love.*

I allow Love to enter at its own speed.

*I ask Love to withdraw, if it must, gently and with compassion, in order
to minimize the pain I might feel at its loss.*

*I release Love at its whim rather than to be, like two back alley mongrels,
locked together in an unholy and painful partnership.*

I ask nothing of Love but to be its partner and reflection.

*I give to Love all that I am, that my very being can be joined to Love, so
that I may experience myself as the Love that passes through me.*

And as Love passes through me, I own it, and it owns me.

*Not as possessions in a world of scarcity, but rather as the ultimate of
preciousness in a sea of bounty, abundance, and possibility.*

*And I know that as Love touches me, I connect to that same Love in all
things, all places, and all people.*

*And I realize that Love is all there is. I realize that I am the all. I
realize I am Love.*

And as I look deeply into your eyes, revealing myself also to you, I the Love that is recognizes myself in you; and I marvel at my own splendor, beauty, and magnificence.

And I know that I am you and you are me.

We are the Love that is. And it is good.

The Schumann Resonances

Seven distinct resonances have been detected by scientists emitting from out of the earth itself. One can only surmise that those seven resonances are simply vibrating and responding in like manner to the vibrations that are coming in to the earth from the cosmos. Like ourselves being human tuning forks, the earth, too resonates according to what reaches it from outside of itself.

The basic Schumann Resonance is said to be 7.83 Hz, and the highest 45 Hz. Normal human brain activity until recently was thought to be limited in a range between 1 and perhaps 30 Hz.

A few years ago the Dalai Lama seconded a number of his best Buddhist meditators to scientific scrutiny. They were invited to engage in deep meditation upon love and compassion.

It was found that these monks achieved brain wave frequencies of around 40 Hz, raising the possibility that it may be possible to achieve complete resonance even with the highest Schumann Resonance at 45 Hz. It could be that this is the vibration that corresponds with the seven ringings, the proverbial 'seventh heaven' spoken of in Islam scripture and inferred in the phrase 'ultimate enlightenment.'

I believe that the Dalai Lama monks were close to achieving resonance with the seventh sacred vibration of creation, and that this frequency is accessible by anyone, given the right direction, commitment, and discipline.

In early November 2010 I was given a speaking opportunity with a local club in Tauranga, New Zealand, that is interested in alternative world views. My opening talk about the seven mystic sounds and the Schumann Resonances was well received, and it seemed that I would soon be giving many other similar talks and seminars dealing with my experiences in the ringings.

Hearing love, seeing love and feeling love.

What do we hear, see and feel with, but love itself?

My Journey with Prostate Cancer

Curiously, two weeks after my first speaking engagement concerning the ringings, my doctor advised me that I possibly had prostate cancer and would require a biopsy ASAP. Shortly before Christmas 2010 I was diagnosed, following the biopsy, with Gleason 7 prostate cancer, was advised that radical treatment was required, and began to wonder just what was going on with my body.

Why me?

Why now?

Finally it occurred to me that this might only be the beginning of my journey, and that the cancer and the ringings might be linked in some way. I decided to forego any invasive treatment for the cancer and try to heal it via my new-found depth of meditation.

For eight months I applied my new meditation technique to my physical well-being, hoping that love would be enough; or at least the amount of love I could self generate would be enough to heal my prostate cancer.

Frustratingly, I found it impossible to hold the seven ringings for more than a short period during that time. It seemed like something just beneath my conscious awareness invariably would pull me back from the source.

During that period, my PSA levels (prostate specific antigen tests) showed a continual rise, suggesting that the prostate cancer was spreading alarmingly. The PSA finally reached a level just beneath 20, and my surgeon told me that if it increased above 20 he would no longer be able to operate, as the cancer would have undoubtedly spread beyond the prostate to the bones by that time.

Desperately seeking further answers, I sought out a traditional Maori healer in my neighborhood who performed a mirimiri body massage on me. She identified a burden of anger in my prostate gland and was even able to announce that my mother had been insane when I was around three years old.

When I heard the word insane I felt like I had been struck with lightning. In an instant I was transported back to the very foundational memory of a childhood trauma event relating to my mother's abusive and insane expression of her anger.

That was the day I saw that my mother was insane and dangerous, the day that I declared I would never let her love me again.

And so it had been right up to the moment of remembering. As a result, throughout my whole life I have been carrying a sense of innocent rage at being so abused for no reason as a child. In that same moment of remembering, I understood the pressure my mother was experiencing at the time, her obvious hormonal imbalance, and the inaccuracy of my own childish observations.

In that same moment I stopped blaming her, and stopped blaming myself for my own ignorance. I had spent most of my life avoiding my mother's love.

Almost instantly, my prostate cancer began receding. Over a period of eight months my PSA test levels nose dived back to around 5 from 20, and my bodily functions relating to the prostate gland stabilized.

I now feel completely healed and rejuvenated.

I can only surmise that my childhood anger predisposed me to a vulnerability in my prostate gland that was repeatedly magnified and triggered by later episodes in my life in which I was left in the throes of victimization and innocent rage originally sourced from my experience around my mother's perceived 'insanity.'

On 24th February 2013, after being away for six years, I attended my mother Ann's 100th birthday party in the USA. For the first time in my life since that experience as a three-year old I was able to genuinely love her. The tears flowed in a way I had never before experienced.

I now firmly believe that the intense trauma we experience as an 'innocent' child at birth may very well be related to unresolved karmic lessons began in former lives, and still waiting to be resolved in this one.

Why else would a perfect God subject the vulnerable and the innocent small children to such a traumatic experience; and at a time when they have no choice but to stand in it?

Even in ignorance we do the will of God, who orchestrates all things.

We are both the condition and the medicine, combined in perfect harmony.

FATHER, DO YOU LOVE ME?

I see fear, anger, and hatred in the faces all around me and I wonder do you love me?

'My son, my love lies hidden beneath the fear, anger, and hatred you see.'

I see people doing horrible things to one another and I wonder do you love me?

'My son, the feelings you hold about what you see remind us both of what we are not.'

People everywhere seem separated and divided along lines of race, culture, religion, and belief system, and I wonder, do you love me?

'My son, only in separation can we experience the bliss of being rejoined; the prodigal son returned home.'

Father, as I follow the rules of my religion I find myself at enmity with my neighbors, and I wonder, do you truly love me?

'My son, there is only one rule in my almighty plan: THERE ARE NO RULES.

Life is about opportunities, not rules. Opportunity to know and be known, to see and be seen, to create and enjoy and to love and be loved.

It is your rules and belief systems that separate you.'

Father, I look for love in the eyes of those I journey with and I see only judgment, rejection and denial; and I wonder do you truly, truly love me?

'My son, of course I love you. LOVE IS ABOUT KNOWING and I wish to know myself. How better to know myself but by SEEING MYSELF IN THE EYES OF ANOTHER ME?

This is PERFECT LOVE, when you humans allow yourselves to be so loved that I can reveal myself through you to all whom you meet, and allow each and everyone to begin to love themselves to the limit, or limitlessness of their choice.

LOVE IS ABOUT CHOICE. Others can choose not to love you, and YOU can choose not to love me. But I cannot choose not to love you.

For you can deny me, but I CANNOT DENY MYSELF.'

Part 2: Karma

What is Karma?

Is karma a punishment, a divine retribution? Contrary to that common belief, I believe karma is a divine toolbox designed to support the spiritual enlightenment and expansion of the soul. It is through the manifestation of karma that we discover who, or what, we are not; ultimately leading towards the realization of who and what we are, and everyone around us. This is a complex and ingenious device that leads us back to God and is reflected in the famous Biblical parable expressed in the story of the prodigal son.

We must be lost, and truly experience being lost, before the universe can rejoice in our homecoming. We must first experience the very worst of the pain we have caused to our other selves before we can be anointed, through compassion, with the ultimate prize of divine love.

I believe that I have lived before in many different lifetimes. During my eternal journey in physicality I have been given, with no handbook or manual, a perfect freedom to think, speak and do, and to explore every conceivable possibility that life offers.

Because I come into each new life in utter forgetfulness and separation, and without any innate understanding of things, and because I have no way I can avoid them, I am given early experiences relating to unresolved karmic lessons brought forward from a past life. The karmic content magnifies and accentuates the actual experience, which may itself be seemingly harmless.

It is likely that our karma settles upon us immediately in the abandonment trauma of our birth, and subsequent abandonment and/or failure episodes in early childhood reinforce the emotional content of the original birth trauma.

These later traumas more consciously experienced by our child selves provide a sort of gateway from the past to the present allowing us one means of resolving our karma through remembering, acceptance, understanding, compassion, and the expression of our love back to the child within.

In the beginning I made choices that are lacking in understanding and more or less based upon my own sense of need or want with no regard to others. I did because I could do. I have no doubt behaved in this way at least in part for many lifetimes. To do this repeatedly throughout a whole life is the mark of a young soul; one experimenting with all the options of life in order to find some meaning or comfort on the journey. In some lives, this manifests in a constant drama of self-gratification at the expense of others.

More advanced souls grow beyond this early forgetfulness quickly, subconsciously remembering and accessing lessons learned in past lives. This is the way all learning commences. We bring pain and suffering to others out of our own ignorance, and so that they (who in reality are we in forgetfulness) might understand the pain and suffering they (we) have caused to others. This is orchestrated perfectly by the divine intelligence.

The second step of this karmic dance may occur during the next life when similar pain is visited upon us, simply to show us what we ourselves have done to others (our other selves); and in this way offering us the opportunity of refining our own existence and spiritual development. We cannot own the wisdom of compassion and the whole experience of love until we have dished out, and received, the worst.

This is not about being punished by those we have punished. In the highest sense, there is no 'other' out there that we abuse, or are abused by. All are connected to the same great I AM, and are simply different manifestations of the same one self. So, what we do to others we do to our own same self. The karmic lessons we acquire teach us how to love ourselves in every manifestation of life, and how to lead other misguided or lost soul fragments back towards the light.

Even what we do in ignorance creates a karmic lesson for us. Intentional abuse creates a powerful lesson. Unintentional abuse creates subtle lessons. This subtle karma sometimes manifests as conditional issues such as genetic weaknesses, malnutrition of one sort or another, and various forms of health challenging pollution. These include chemical additives in our food, pesticides, weedicides, fungicides, genetically modified foods, and nutrient deficient soils.

Most of these conditional issues come about as a result of the best of intentions by people (the other selves) somewhere down the line before us. Many of them can be resolved by conscious intention now. First, we must recognize an issue and apply a kind of conscious awareness to the issue that was lacking by those who originally created the faulty science behind the issue.

We can in some degree heal the affected parts of our bodies by proper nutrition, exercise and life style; and perhaps contribute to a wider understanding within the community of the causes and cures for many of the maladies resulting.

Ultimately, we will realize the perfect karmic balance of all things; we will stand and face our karmic lessons; and from that time forward we will be able to begin living the life of the Gods. In short, karma is the way and the means of developing an individual and personal Godhood through time.

Karma is the wonderful tool of spiritual advancement that shows us how we feel when we abuse another us. Without karma we would never know compassion. Without compassion we would never know love. Without love we would never know life. So, without karma, we would never truly know ourselves.

Accept that everything is exactly as it was meant to be; your circumstances right now are a perfect reflection of all the choices you have made; and your choices right now will manifest the shape and content of your future. Choose wisely, and play hard.

No one in the medical profession will ever call a remarkable recovery from cancer a cure. There is a prevalent mentality in the profession that such a patient shouldn't really make any long-term plans. Sooner of later the unwanted visitor will return, and often with a vengeance.

In my own case, upon learning of my cancer, two distinct fears surfaced immediately. The first of those was the fear that through medical intervention I would become impotent and lose access to my sexuality, and perhaps also become incontinent for the rest of my life; the both of which made that 'rest of my life' significantly less palatable than it had seemed previously.

The second fear, of course, was that it appeared that my life was giving notice to me that I was facing a much earlier use-by date than anticipated. Time suddenly became a lot more important to me. I had to take a long hard look at how I wanted to spend what time I had remaining. Did I want to spend my time groveling to the medical profession hoping for a few more months, weeks, days, or hours of suffering, or did I want to spend my life in my own power for as long as I possibly could; and take my medical chances involved in not treating the cancer.

After discovering the love of God in my meditation experiences this became a no brainer. My work clearly was to discover myself completely before I died. My worst fear has been that I might die before I live. My hope has been that I might live before I die. So, I chose to spend my remaining quality time in truly searching for myself within, and in searching for those persons that might come into my life who will help me to see, to enjoy, and to love life even more while it lasts.

We're all going to die sometime. So why worry about the when? I want to live powerfully, and perhaps die powerfully, fully aware of myself, who I have come to be, who I have become and who I have loved. In facing my fear of death, and resolving my karma around that fear, the universe has given me a new lease on life. It still may be my karmic lesson that I will eventually die of prostate cancer at some time in the future. In facing up to this reality with open eyes, I have purchased the keys to the mind, heart, and soul of God.

And regardless of what the future might bring, I am eternally grateful for the opportunity to finally be the real me that has been waiting all these years to come out and play from within the revolving door of karma.

Karma – and what we do about it – makes the man.

But if a man happens to find himself he has a mansion which he can inhabit with dignity all the days of his life.

James Michener

THE REVOLVING DOOR

We've passed from out another life
Where all things are as just before:
Where all things be that ever *were,*
Till we step through the revolving door.

To come from place that seems so vast
Requires our soul to entertain
The thought that when we be a part
Experience we a new domain.

We enter, then, the revolving door,
And 'round we go by our own choice;
Pretending that we're lost from love
So we can find and then rejoice.

Sometimes when lost within the door
In dizziness we fall to floor;
Till we recall the game we play
And choose again in game to stay.

The rounding door has made us spin
And given need to look within;
For only when we conquer doubt
Can we then risk to look without.

Round and round we go in search
Of that for which we've come to face
Till dare we leap from rounding door
And step into a third new place.

Its then we see through door outside
Where we've come from upon this ride,
And see our game from inside out,
We then can see what life's about.

We are the eyes that look upon,
And, that which passes in our view.
We must be both, and even more;
What joins us we can be that, too.

How can we be duality?
And even more, to be all three?
I must be you, and you be me;
And, that which uses us to see.

So when you feel you're lost in hell
Remember you're the door as well.
We lose ourselves so we'll be found
When finally we stop spinning round.

No longer lost in rounding door
The hard part of the game is through;
What joyous paths lie now before
I travel, now, with love, in you.

Until the day our love transcends
Our earthly bounds and this life ends.
In death we simply take a rest;
When tired, we can't play our best.

We're back from where we started from;
The very place from which we've come,
Where all is known and all's been done:
We're not a part, *but back as one.*

We rest until we want still more
To play again in the revolving door.

The Origins of Karma

The classical form of karma is almost a cliché. I have done something to another soul fragment in a past life; and they are returning the 'favor' to me in this life so that I can know how horrible it can feel. For example, I may have been an abusive parent in a past life. This time around I am the abused child. This may very well be a drama played out within a particular soul group, always more or less interacting with the same group of soul fragments.

The unfolding drama plays out in this way because the identity overlay (the ability to subconsciously recognize familiar souls) deepens the karmic experience offering a purer lesson and a cleaner karmic outcome. The soul group common karmic memory ensures that unused karma will never be lost or forgotten- even through many, many incarnations- until it is resolved, and the prize of compassion is finally won.

Not all karma comes in the form of an immediate reversed circumstance revisiting us. If we have failed to resolve a karmic lesson offered in our past life, the same lesson will be continually repeated throughout this lifetime and succeeding lifetimes until we own the experience and the lesson and finally resolve our behavior around that type of situation.

We also in all likelihood occasionally take on the unresolved karma of our direct ancestors. We are karmically linked via our ethereal field and our DNA to all who have come before us. In a very real sense we <u>are</u> our ancestors, and they are us. The closer to us in terms of succession, the more powerful these unresolved ancestral karmic responsibilities manifest.

It seems almost certain that genetic weaknesses carry unresolved karma from our ancestors, and that we can actually alter our DNA by resolving our karma around those issues.

This may very well be one of the reasons our deceased ancestors choose to hang around us for a time before moving on with their own karmic spiritual journey. They encourage us to resolve our own karma which may very well help resolve theirs in the process.

Until we finally realize our true nature in the ability of shaping our own experience through our choices, we undoubtedly create numerous karmic lessons in each lifetime. So, many of my own karmic tests have been cemented in and added on to my original karma this time around. I have made a lot of 'bad' choices, and have seemingly 'hurt' a lot of other spiritual 'children.' I never meant to hurt anyone. I just didn't know any better.

Fortunately, there is much that we can do in this lifetime to resolve this type of karma without having to carry it along into the next lifetime. Much is said of forgiveness. However, forgiveness is only a halfway house to resolution. No one can really forgive us of anything. So long as we or they think there is something that needs to be forgiven, there can be little or no movement towards resolution; as one party or the other continues to hold on to an illusionary debt of one kind or another.

Everything we do or have done is perfectly measured out by our divine self as a tool of karmic expression.

Sometimes we make choices that provide another person the perfect karmic lesson for that person to take on in that moment.

Sometimes we make choices that lay the foundation for our own karmic growth.

And sometimes either we or they choose to accept the karmic lesson graciously, and in the process move on to a higher spiritual consciousness. Because we are all ageless and eternal, neither we, nor they, can in truth hurt, or be hurt, by anyone.

And the way we resolve the karma we have created in the present life is simply to stand in and own the emotional consequences of our choices without blaming either ourself or the other person for the pain that might accompany the experience.

The key is to accept that we are neither innocent nor blameworthy, that all things unfold following the will (choice) of

God, and that *YOU ARE A PART OF GOD*. Conscious awareness embraces karma and resolves it at every opportunity.

Destiny or Free Choice?

What is the essential quality of life? When I look upon this question from the viewpoint of my false ego self, it appears to be an impossible riddle to answer. If there is predetermined destiny, then there cannot be free choice. Conversely, if there is any sense of free choice, how can there be destiny?

Likewise, when considering all the dysfunction, violence, murder and mayhem in the world, it is almost impossible to consider that God, through destiny, arranged things in this way. From a perspective of separation between me and God, it would appear that the two elements cannot possibly co-exist. It might also appear that there can be no element of destiny.

I must alter my perspective in order to realize the truth and resolve the question. In actuality, I am a partially realized piece of a perfect God. Thus, it is I (the God in me) who has created every outcome by my choice and by my word. As a piece of God I have absolute choice in the manifestation of my will, and have been a party to every choice ever made throughout all creation. And even as the universe is ordered down to the tiniest detail, it has been predetermined by my own divine choice.

Very cool, indeed.

I believe there is a continuing battle raging between our powers of free choice and destiny. Humankind through its God-given genius continually strives to avoid and deny its karmic lessons, and God continually creates new avenues of communication between our unresolved karma of the past and our present experience.

We can run, but we cannot hide. Our karma runs with us, ultimately to be faced, resolved, and learned from. Only then can we achieve the wholeness and vibrant health awaiting us in God's embrace. That is our destiny, which will always manifest sooner or

later, no matter how hard – in ignorance and fear – we try to avoid
it.

Whenever we face an important, difficult, and painful task, isn't
it always easier in the end to do it now and get it over with? Why
would it be any different with our karmic lessons? In this case, not
only does the pain end, but we surely will find treasure buried right
there at the source of our perceived pain, if only we look. Therein
lay our ticket to bliss, a pathway straight toward the love of God.

There is calmness beneath the eye of a hurricane. There is also
calmness in the 'we' beneath the 'I'.

We are healed of a suffering only by experiencing it to the full.

Marcel Proust

DO WE CHOOSE TO LOVE?

We think we choose to love someone
And that's the way our love's begun;
This simple truth I share with you-
It's love from what we've all come from.

For love waits there within us all
Just waiting for another call;
We hide from love so we won't fall,
Our disappointments to forestall.

The choice is this, and always was,
To run from love; and just because
It hurts so much when it seems gone;
Its then we know for what we long!

We look for reasons not to love,
And when we find one, give a shove;
So choice is just a tool we use
To part from love and self-abuse.

The universe has made the choice
To be, and love is its sole voice;
It chooses us whatever we do
And waits for us to let it through.

Are we the love that stands in wait?
Will ego take us for its mate?
Will ego love? What is our fate?!
It's choice that makes us hesitate.

Dare we stand in love anew?
A path that's taken by so few,
To deny love is just not you,
Your choice is really, 'What to do?'

Mastering the Ego

We stumble and fall before our challenges not because we are not big enough to conquer them. It is because our ego, our false self based upon our past, does not know who we really are. The ego only knows and allows success 'by accident' and/or spontaneity, not by design.

In the world of our ego, success is measured by the amount of pain we can avoid, rather than as the amount of love we can experience through our own multidimensional divine self. The ego is a type of watchdog designed to help us avoid unnecessary pain.

The ego also is the basis for our sense of separation - that then allows us to experience all the other stuff of creation. The ego embraces all our past experiences repeatedly underscoring our temporary separation from God, and giving us a space from within which we can then journey back towards God. However, that journey begins only when we remember that there is a God to journey back to.

Mastering the ego is about remembering, and about balance.

Why do we not immediately rise up and claim our inheritance? It is because our worst fear is not that we may fail again. Our worst fear is that we just might remember our own true magnificence, requiring us to sacrifice all those little bits of ego by which we have so long been, almost comfortably, identifying ourselves with.

In fact, our little ego has been running the show for so long that it truly thinks it is the boss. And until YOU decide to take control once and for all, you will continue to be a slave to your worst fears, accepting as your truth the meager crumbs of truth that ego allows to escape through it from under the tightly closed door of love.

Don't you remember from your childhood? You are not good enough, worthy enough, big enough, smart enough, or wise enough to be loved; or to amount to anything significant.

Why would your ego sign off on a choice that would surely lead to more abandonment, disappointment, and rejection?

Why would your ego sign off on a choice that would destroy its only power of control, which is the final choice *not to love?*

That is the only power the ego has, and it will bitterly oppose any attempt you make to take it away. After all, who are YOU, to know any better?

I am here to tell you that you are the universe, and that your ego is your servant, not your master.

No man can serve two masters...

Matthew 6, v.24

How do we fast forward our own spiritual growth? How do we find, meet, and keep the love our soul desires? It's really very simple. We must turn and face our worst fears.

We chose those challenges in the beginning for the very purpose of rapid growth towards ascension. They have materialized with the assistance, and by the imagination of, our own ego. Once we bring the illumination of love to bear upon them, they must by design disintegrate and fall away.

And through understanding, we gain an incredible new tool of compassion; both for ourselves and for all we meet in love.

We know our past and rely upon it for our definition.

This reeks of death, worshipping what has gone before, and blind unto that which falls upon us in the moment.

135

THE EGO

The ego is an awesome tool when in its proper place.
It helps us to discern in life, and meet things face to face.

For choosing what we want to be creates a place to stand,
And gifts us our 'aloneness' for to love a sharing hand.

We can't be 'found' until we're lost, a mystery of life.
Our peace means nothing to our souls until we've been through strife.

So honor ego for its role in helping us forget,
That we be spirit, through and through, and will return to it.

Our ego is the gatekeeper between that life and this.
It gives us legs to stand in both, experiencing true bliss.

The ego sets the standards that we then attempt attain.
Without those standards calling us, in past we might remain.

My ego, too, deserves my love, a hug from time to time.
Because it's when we stand alone we can then intertwine.

So when we honor ego, that which parts us from all others,
Discover we the thing that lets us stand together brothers.

When ego finds its rightful place, towards love, it too, will bow.
And offer us our choices, not with whom, but rather how.

Remembering Our Childhood Trauma

Those early childhood experiences, existing outside the realm of verbal understanding, can be very difficult to uncover and resolve. It is most helpful if the pilgrim is able to access some degree of his or her own innate wisdom source in order to navigate back through his or her life.

One needn't be fully enlightened, but it is almost imperative that one is at least on a journey towards that end. Understanding what must be true as opposed to what cannot possibly be true is also helpful. And a good question is worth a million trivial answers.

Brandon Bays, in her wonderful book *The Journey* offers some very effective ways to resolve those troublesome childhood trauma memories, and thus remove any personal encumbrance against loving and being loved. Brandon describes her own journey in healing a uterine cancer the size of a basketball in six weeks, simply by accessing, and resolving, the childhood experience at the foundation of her jealous anger. It was while reading The Journey (after my prostate cancer had receded) that I finally realized with no uncertainty the importance of my own 'remembering.'

Dr. Deepak Chopra, author of *Quantum Healing*, has done extensive work in proving the apparent existence of cellular memory and the importance of accessing and resolving repressed trauma memories in healing life threatening diseases such as cancer.

The popular memoir *A Change of Heart* describes the experiences of Claire Sylvia who underwent a heart/lung transplant. After surgery she began having lucid dreams of a young man who, at one point declared 'I will always be with you.' She began to crave chicken nuggets and to ride on a motorcycle. Ultimately, she researched and found the family of her donor. They confirmed her heart and lung had come from their son who had died riding a motorcycle with chicken nuggets firmly held within his leather jacket.

If all memories are held within our cells, or if our cells can provide some sort of Stargate or time warp to the past, and if suppressed emotional experiences can lead to life threatening illnesses, they surely will interfere with the connective tissue of love in relationship.

The work of both Brandon Bays and Deepak Chopra offers evidence that childhood traumas carry forward a predisposition to reject love with others and reject connection to our own higher self.

Prayer, meditation, past life regression, hypnotherapy, psychic intervention, deep bodywork, and kinesiology are all potentially effective methods of retrieving and resolving those internalized childhood emotions. The important element in any such healing is finding access to the 'feeling' part of the brain instead of trying to analyze the problem through the verbal tools of the intellectual part of the brain.

The left brain is the home of most verbal and non-verbal memory, but as long as we attempt to recover those memories via language, we are doomed to failure. It falls to a specialized part of the brain to make an intuitive bridge to the feeling part of the brain, and perhaps to the heart, in order to uncover those repressed memories and emotions.

In completely remembering and resolving them our cells and/or body field can release the limiting belief systems of our childhood and allow us to love and connect freely once again.

We hold the wisdom to release the wounded child from its karmic chains.

God mediates in the conversation between ourselves across time, if only we listen.

The 'Must be So' Self-Judgment

The Divine Spirit from which we all have come is intentional. First there was the Word, then the manifestation of the Word. Cause and effect, intention and manifestation, are the fundamental building blocks of all creation.

At birth, we have come directly from this absolute world of cause and effect. Our caregivers take the place of the divine father/mother experienced in spirit, and we naturally believe them to be a physical manifestation of that same vibration. They are all of that, but usually slumbering in a sort of deep forgetfulness. This continues to be a part of our belief system until we begin to realize that the world of mankind, created as it was with free choice and the power not to be, does not always express its divine nature.

And yet, until we come to that realization, we quite correctly believe that everything that we experience is caused by a divine intention imbued with the appropriate karmic essence.

I believe absolutely that this is so. Undoubtedly the karmic lessons we receive in early childhood are a reflection of the karma we have acquired and brought through from past lives to experience and heal in this one. That does not make them any easier to resolve. No doubt we have been the abuser in many past lives. It follows that our childhood experiences of trauma and abuse are the very things our soul needs in order to purge and correct our spiritual misadventures in past lives.

I don't believe there is any judgment or punishment being meted out by the divine consciousness. I believe that these childhood experiences are planted in our psyche as an opportunity to finally face up to our karma, stand in it fully as conscious adults, receive the lessons with their full emotional charge, and then add them to our own karmic treasure chest of the soul.

It's never been about punishment. It's all about growth of the soul, and learning how to stand in unconditional love.

And neither does karma necessarily reflect a wrong directed towards or from any individual soul in a past life. At the highest level of vibration we are all the same soul. Karma is distributed in exact measure not for what we have done to others, but according to what we have done to our 'selves' - our other selves - in a past life.

Hence it is not a punishment, but rather, a lesson.

At any rate, when we are abused by our caregivers in any way, whether it be in a physical, sexual, verbal, or emotional way, our first and lasting response will likely be to assume that this is precisely what we deserve. In the perfect vibration from which we recently came, all things were in karmic balance. Thus, we are very likely to attach to this experience the 'must be so' energy of guilt and complicity, without having any idea of just what, exactly, we have done to deserve this.

In the Christian Biblical sense, this is the proverbial 'sins of the fathers' passed on to the children.

Maybe even original sin.

Our problems begin when we forget that 'it must be so'. Things present in that way so that we can accept and resolve the karmic lesson held within.

It is that it is. Stop running, and deal with it. Now.

Escaping from the 'Forever' Moment

The eternal spirit is beyond time. The great something/nothing is eternal and infinite. Because there is nothing outside of itself by which to measure and experience change and movement, to the great 'I am' the concept of passing time cannot exist. From this great nothingness, silence, emptiness and darkness emit the vibrations that eventually manifest as the energies and particles of creation.

Only when these energies and particles take motion moving from one 'space' into another does time show up as an experiential phenomenon.

So time came into being only after vibration ('the Word') brought forth the illusion of the universe as something real and moving. And then it remained for the great magician to forget itself enough in order for it to perceive and experience the illusion of itself.

Before our conception we were one with the divine. This meant that at least on one level we were experiencing ourselves 'out of time' in a space that seemed ageless and eternal, and in which, on a divine level, nothing ever changed. The mighty Solomon of old might have been having a forever moment when he declared, 'There is nothing new under the sun.'

When we emerge at birth, we have come directly from that forever place. Time passes slowly as young children because we are slow to perceive change or understand what it means. We continue to live in the forever moment until we begin to grasp the meaning and direction of the changes we perceive around us.

I believe that very young children experience what is happening at the moment as what will always be happening. This explains why a child can hold and express a painful experience for a long time; sometimes seemingly for ages after the fact, and why childhood fears seem so real and intransigent.

There is a magic to this childish sense of timelessness, and also a curse. Children can play ecstatically outside of the worry and drama of time, but can also become trapped in any number of forever moments. Science and medicine are beginning to accept that our bodies somehow manage to store, hold, or access all our experiences in life somewhere in or through our bodies. It may well be that the memories of past lives are held or accessed through our bodies as well.

Those memories can be anywhere. They may be in every single cell throughout our body, they may be stored in our ethereal body field, and/or specific types of memories may be organ specific. And we may somehow be accessing those memories across time. There is a huge body of new evidence that suggests that unresolved childhood traumas stored somewhere within our living field can interfere with the natural healing and growth processes and create a predisposition for the development later in life of phobias, hang-ups, and life threatening illnesses centered in the areas in which the unresolved memories seem to be held.

In my own personal experience, and oftentimes in the experience of others whom I have coached or counseled, we easily recall aspects of these childhood traumas, thinking we have resolved them in the memory thereof; only later to discover that there has been a deeper layer of emotion hidden there which we were unaware of. I believe that when we experience trauma in those very early formative years, we in some way stamp the memory with an aspect of our forever consciousness.

In other words, we create a story around that emotion that reads something like this: *This is a terrible experience. I've been abandoned, (or rejected, punished blamelessly, taken from, made wrong, or judged harshly) and it feels like this is how it will be forever.*

We then imbue the memory with this sense of forever until we can resurrect the whole memory and correct it by relegating it back to the single moment in time it deserves. The reason we make such a big deal of it at the time of first experience is that we really feel that we are trapped in the unfortunate experience forever. This is akin to a sense of eternal damnation.

We might as well be in hell. Maybe that *is* hell, or at least an introductory sample. And it keeps coming back throughout our life until we deal with it.

Recently I began to question why it seemed that I have repeatedly seemed to sabotage myself over and over just when I was about to succeed brilliantly at one endeavor or another. This book is one example. It was begun fifteen years ago and still holds much of the earlier contributions.

I suspected that there may be other 'must be so' self-judgments or 'forever moments' that I was hanging on to subconsciously without realizing it.

I returned to an early childhood memory that has tormented me many times. I found myself as a toddler crawling around and playing happily in the attic of a large home surrounded by all my brothers, sister, and numerous cousins. Suddenly, they all seemed to disappear, obviously having been called to supper. I realized that I was alone and abandoned. And I began bawling my head off.

I've experienced this memory many times. However, this time around I looked deeper into the feeling part of the memory and discovered that horrible forever feeling. What frightened me the most was the feeling that I would be abandoned forever. And as a direct result of that childhood experience, throughout my life I realize that I have repeatedly expected to be abandoned in many of the activities and relationships that I have undertaken.

Once I realized this, I was overcome with sympathy and compassion for the helpless young fellow that I was, and began showering him with all the love that I could muster. Then with him I quickly relegated the memory back to the single moment in time that it deserved. Almost instantly I began experiencing myself as a completely new person; unshackled from something I had been, in ignorance, dragging around with me for my whole life. And replacing that niggling feeling of impending failure or abandonment, I now feel a sense of absolute and infinite power.

I have finally broken through to a solid state of being-ness; and this is being reflected in every part of my life. Even my tennis game has stepped up to an awesome new level.

It may well be that we have been hanging on to the unresolved issues of past lives almost forever. This concept adds another element of credibility to the forever feeling and lasting strength of the emotion. The younger we are at the time of the event, the greater the likelihood that the event becomes a forever emotion constantly rising up throughout our life until it is healed and resolved. As we grow older we become less susceptible to single events, but continue to remain vulnerable to the forever aspect of repeating sequences.

For example, a single experience of abuse at a young age can affect a person for a lifetime, or perhaps many lifetimes; depending upon whether he/or she is the victim or the perpetrator, and depending upon whether we accept our karmic lesson or not.

A single experience of sexual abuse between the ages of 6-10, traumatic as it may be, is often relatively easy to resolve later in life; because the verbal and feeling memories of it may be more easily accessed. However, if that abuse continues over a considerable length of time, it almost certainly attracts the forever moment of emotional feeling; absolutely requiring the victim to revisit, absorb completely, and reframe the forever element in his/her adult emotions before the underlying trauma event can be resolved and healed.

It may be that we must fully experience the horror of the abuse once again before we are able to conjure up enough love to make our injured child feel whole and well. And it may take many journeys back to the source of the trauma before your child self feels loved enough to let it go.

It seems clear to me that we are never given more than we can handle at any given moment. We may not handle it this time around, but that is a question of choice rather than ability. We remain free to make 'bad' choices throughout our life. In fact, we *need* to make a number of 'bad' choices during our journey of spiritual growth. Otherwise we would never learn compassion and grow.

Adult spin-offs from the forever moment include the constant feeling that you are about to be or going to be abandoned, that you are always going to be alone, and/or that you become jealous with or about anyone of the same sex (in a heterosexual relationship) that relates in any way with your partner. Partners seriously affected with the forever moment often attempt to sequester themselves and their partner away from the mainstream of social life in an attempt to minimize the possibilities of abandonment.

This ultimately results in an opposite outcome as the sequestered individual generally 'escapes' at some point back into life. If unresolved in this lifetime, the forever moment carries the unresolved emotional trauma with it forward into future lives, always putting itself forward in the spiritual queue intended for resolution and growth.

We can resolve and heal those forever emotional statements by remembering and re-experiencing the emotion itself in its fullest and most complete aspect. In allowing ourselves to experience it fully, we take ownership over it as ours, we accept the emotional lesson held therein, and empower ourselves to do what we like with it from that time forward. It then becomes a simple task to re-file the memory in its wholeness away from the negative and limiting impact it has had up to now in our lives and place it as a new tool into our treasure chest of wisdom.

Once re-filed and re-framed in this way, the childhood experience becomes available to us to be used in helping other persons who may have had the same childhood experiences and be experiencing the same kind of phenomena in the present as a result. In re-filing the childhood emotion, our original trauma memory changes from being an emotional scourge constantly interfering in all our adult relationships, to being the basis and source wisdom for a new-found sense of compassion and love for others; not the least of which is our own inner child.

If your forever moment is an unresolved issue brought forward from a past life, as many are, it does not require you to inquire into those past lives in order to heal the emotional trauma that you carry as a result. Simply in accepting and experiencing the resulting emotional content that we are given fully, we fulfill our karmic duty, then releasing us to climb further up our own karmic ladder towards becoming our full, 'cleansed,' and educated higher self.

Unless science can in some way prove otherwise, I believe that the entire concept of time is simply a divine contrivance by which the great I AM entertains itself in the illusion of separation, change, and movement. Thus, all times co-exist in the moment (there really is nothing else), and your former child-self, and all your previous karmic experience, remains instantly connectable through your higher self. You can engage with that child or former self whenever you like in order to reassure, advise, counsel, and love him or her in the very way that will transform the foundational experience from one of distress into higher understanding.

It really is as simple as that. Remember deeply. Become that troubled child again. Dare to feel the whole experience again, just as it was to you then. Look for and grasp the forever moment feeling in its wholeness.

Own it as yours.

And then simply relegate it to the single moment in time that it deserves. And love that child that you were as the awesome, innocent, and perfect being that he or she was/is.

No more blame, no more guilt, and no more self-judgment required.

If we can access the child of our past across time, so then we can access elements of our future self. So, why not project yourselves into the future, check in with your future self to ascertain how you are feeling then, and bring that back to the moment as an added surety or confidence booster, knowing that the issue you are dealing with now will surely be healed soon?

Magic happens only when we acknowledge and accept it. And there is no better time to begin than right now. After all, that's all there is.

I recently read an account of an investigation of prayer held within the book The Intention Experiment. Two hundred patients with a similar prognosis were chosen in a major hospital and divided into a test group and a control group. A well known faith healer was hired to pray every day for each individual in the test group. The personal details of each prayer recipient were given to the faith healer.

After a period of six months, each group was examined to compare what, if any, difference occurred between the two groups. The group that had been prayed for showed a very significant benefit from the remote prayer. There were fewer deaths, fewer days in hospital, and an undeniable overall improvement in quality of life. This is not the first study showing that prayer works.

The remarkable thing about this study is that, while the patients were universally treated in exactly the same way between 1990 and 1993, the healing prayer was applied to the test group only in the year 2000. Thus, the prayer was able to reach back in time and affect the patients involved retroactively.

Clearly, if what we think, say, and do in the present can affect the past, it clearly must create our future in ways that it is almost impossible to fully comprehend. And this account gives further credence to the healing power of loving our 'former' child self in his/her pain.

If you are a parent of young children, or are contemplating starting a family, I strongly recommend that you consider the import of these revelations to your own situation and how it impacts on the children that might at some point be involved. Being a parent is no small matter. And how you parent shapes the experiences, character, and emotional qualities of your children.

Your input can speed up or slow down your child's spiritual development, depending solely upon whether or not you are aware of your role in that development.

It is not enough to have a child and then separate yourself from their needs, which are full time and monumental in proportion to the modern family resources of time available.

The concept of the modern nuclear family has proven itself bankrupt in so many ways. It has been functionless for decades since the 'mother' was left to raise the family. And now, with so many families depending upon two incomes in order to survive, there is no substance of real child support remaining.

As a result, the fabric of our society is being rent apart by the constant emotional explosions of its unresolved parts. At the heart of all things, it is the pent up, unexpressed, and unresolved childhood trauma emotions of the multitudes that are causing all the violence, confrontation, and disconnection being experienced in the world today.

How wonderful it would be if we could, through genuine parenting, help our young children resolve their childhood traumas, even those carrying over from past lives, in their early years. This then would open up the possibility of a long and fruitful life filled with spiritual growth, unconditional love, the appreciation of beauty and perfection, and divine gratitude for the very opportunity of being.

God will wait forever for us to resolve our issues and grow up.

How much time have *you* got?

The Link between early Abandonment & Later Ownership

Tribal structures cater to a community wide effort at parenting the children. In a sense, the children belong to the whole tribe and everyone takes some responsibility in their upbringing. Intimate relationships, should they exist, may be simple or complex. Some cultures allow easy transfer of affections from one partner to another partner. In other cultures the provision of food, shelter, protection and security becomes paramount in distinguishing relationships. But even in a harsh and uncompromising environment the children represent the future well-being of the tribe and are considered a tribal asset.

In most primitive tribal cultures true parenting is passed over to the elders who act as both parent and teacher to the young while the younger adults busy themselves in providing the necessities of life and making new babies.

In today's western societies, the need for the necessities of life is greatly diminished. In most modern countries there is at least a modicum of social support available for the sick, homeless and hungry. A woman no longer needs a man to support her and/or her children as before; and thus the physical need for committed long-term relationship is greatly diminished.

This does not make this a happy or healthy state of affairs. To the contrary, the modern nuclear family represents a miserable social failure. When laid against the present deepening disparity between the rich and the poor and the poverty consciousness that accompanies high unemployment and widespread debt slavery, it appears even more important that the intimacy that preludes pregnancy converts into a long term commitment to provide for and support the resulting family unit.

This is at least partially catered to in most jurisdictional family law.

However, even after the children are raised, educated and sent out to meet the world there seems to remain a social agenda pointing towards long term commitment and a sense of relationship ownership that outlives the need for raising a family. At a time when fully 50% of all marriages fail for one reason or another, even the childless – or newly child free – persons continue to seek out that perfect 'one', the soul mate that will love them unconditionally forever. And at a time when many mature persons have the means to live the life of their dreams and yet continue to grasp for the security of a long term commitment.

Why is this?

Why do we not unconditionally seek out the love and friendship of a host of personal relationships, broadening the sense of our own personal tribe so to speak, and connecting through love to anyone and everyone ready to reflect our own value?

I believe the answer to this question lies buried within our earliest childhood traumas. More precisely to that earliest lucid childhood abandonment memory and the forever moment that we attached to the experience. Most persons continue to fear a recurring abandonment experience based upon the childhood event and spend a considerable amount of adult energy either in running away from the emotional content at every opportunity, or in contracting in a long term commitment as part and parcel of a late-in-life relationship; at the very time when they could be having the time of their lives with a wealth of positive social interactions and connections. It is our fear of the unresolved 'forever' abandonment expectation that continues to drive our need for security and commitment later in life, robbing many of us of this wonderful opportunity as elders to connect with the many in our lives including the young, the working middle ages and our own social peers. At a time when we could be and should be free, we often succumb to those unresolved emotional chains that have been weighing us down and imprisoning us in an emotional dungeon throughout our entire life.

We choose our chains and would fight to the death to defend them.

The 'Never, Ever' Declaration

As we grow we adapt to change as rapidly as we can. We learn to appreciate change, movement, and time-keeping around us. We begin to succumb to the pressures and necessities of time, and more or less learn to move with it. If we don't, we feel ourselves to be always out of step; and society punishes us savagely.

Coming as we do at birth away from infinite power and connection and into powerlessness, forgetfulness, and separation, it is inevitable that we begin to experience repeated episodes of personal failure in our new life. In the beginning we can do nothing. What we see and perceive has no meaning to us, so there is nothing we 'would' do about it even if we could.

Only when we begin to attach meaning to our surroundings do we begin to attempt to attain some mastery, or control, over them.

As it were, our ability to master new movements and activities is directly tied to our body's rate of growth and expansion. Nonetheless, our blossoming new desires and intentions seem to proceed with 'a mind of their own.'

Unfortunately, our emotional needs continually seem to outstrip our abilities to meet or understand them ourselves.

For a very long time those new desires and aspirations seem to condemn us to repeated failure; until our body catches up to our desires and provides the means to accomplish the tasks, and our spirit acquires the understanding to deal with them emotionally.

In the meantime, we grow through a veritable minefield of emotional failures imbued with the forever moment or the must be so self judgment to one degree or another.

Ultimately these forever moments and must be so judgments will probably develop sooner or later into some form of the never, ever declaration. This can manifest in at least two different aspects.

On the one hand, it may relate to our own sense of accomplishment later in life, wherein we either fail to take on worthwhile projects in which we believe we will not be successful, or we subconsciously sabotage those activities.

It may well be that this sense of imminent failure is a hangover from in-completions in past lives, and those karmic in-completions are then emotionally 'tacked on' to the abandonment or guilt experiences of our childhood this time around.

Whatever may be the source of the emotion, should our childhood failures be reinforced in any significant way by our parents or caregivers, there is the very strong likelihood that we begin to feel like we will 'never' be good enough to accomplish anything of importance in life. As an example, should we identify ourselves with our repeated failures, we could easily 'rubber stamp' ourselves with a sense that we will never be good enough, smart enough, strong enough or agile enough to accomplish anything of real worth. And if that sticks we will become our own worst enemy continually sabotaging our own best efforts at getting it right.

Eventually, as we begin to understand the world around us, we begin to sense the 'worldly unfairness' of it all (at least from the viewpoint of the present life cycle). This sense of unfairness often then manifests as unresolved and deep-rooted anger (innocent rage), and/or an ongoing sense of victimhood later in our life; particularly if we perceive that we are not being supported in our attempts, are being thwarted in some way by a caregiver, or are being judged wrongly while 'innocent.'

As a result we may make a declaration to ourselves subconsciously that we will never, ever love this or that person again, or anyone later in life that exhibits or contributes to a like experience. It may even lead to a subconscious decision never to show or express our true emotions to anyone. Once the inner child decides that a caregiver, other person, or activity is hurtful, dangerous, or wrongly judgmental they will likely never allow themselves to love those persons, do that type of activity, or submit to that kind of judgment ever again.

The never, ever declaration is simply a further more complex and refined aspect of the forever moment turned upside down with one of the first inklings of conscious intention. And it may be our first attempt at exercising a sort of perverted and counter-productive sense of control into our lives.

Spinoffs later in life from the never, ever declaration include the ongoing resentment felt in being manipulated or told what to do, the propensity to continually be late to appointments as a means of at least feeling some degree of control, and passive aggressive controlled anger; slice-and-dice behaviors that chip away at our relationships despite our best efforts at loving.

My early childhood experience with my mother's perceived insanity lead me to declare that I would never, ever allow her to love me; and I subconsciously followed that declaration for most of my life. It was only in reframing the memory with my adult understanding that I was able to stop blaming her for her own expressed anger, and stop blaming myself for sabotaging so many of my adult relationships. This was the key to healing my prostate cancer.

Curiously, it was my mother's healthy but inappropriate expressions of her anger that has allowed her to stay alive and relatively healthy to the ripe old age of a hundred. Unfortunately, projecting her anger on us children has had quite a different impact on us.

The never, ever declaration is very similar to the forever moment. When I experienced my own abandonment as a toddler, I attached the forever moment to that memory. To be always expecting abandonment naturally led into a subconscious sense that I would never, ever really succeed in business or in relationship.

Why?

Because I would always be abandoned in some way when I needed assistance or love.

In looking back now, I realize that I have been subtly sabotaging myself just before the moment of victory in so many different ways that it makes the mind boggle. And in realizing this in myself, and removing the forever moment and the never, ever declaration from this filed memory, I now experience myself expecting to be successful in everything I do. And the universe is giving me exactly what I expect. This is not about hanging my hat on any particular expectation in the future. It is about being that expectation in the present. I feel successful, therefore I am. In the end, it's all about feelings; and all about feelings in the now.

There is no other place.

The 'now' speaks in feelings.

Are you listening?

God loves us right now and is never, ever going to stop.

The Conflict that Kills

Clearly, the combinations of the must be so guilt we carry, the forever moment that attaches to us throughout our life, and the never, ever declarations against our own success, or in anger over our innocence, create an incredible inner conflict upon our soul. We cannot be both guilty and innocent in and of the same event. This is a type of insanity that nearly every person has to deal with at some point in our lives.

Usually, we choose either one or another of these aspects around which we build a coping mechanism, and continue to project that aspect throughout our life until it is resolved. The primary aspect is much easier to identify than the more hidden secondary. For example, this conflict may manifest on the surface simply as the 'I'm not good enough' guilt and abandonment trip. Or it may show up as the 'poor me' victim role wherein we carry with us through life a quiet but profound innocent rage; expecting the universe to make it right for us.

Usually the secondary aspect will show up only after the primary one has been identified and at least partly resolved. With time, patience and courage, these inner conflicts can easily be resolved step by step by identifying the deep and hidden feeling aspects of each of the memory events, or each aspect of the same event.

But in some instances individuals will continue to carry both or all aspects with them through life, continually being in conflict with oneself at every level. In these cases it is no great wonder then that many persons develop split personalities, schizophrenia, bipolar tendencies, ADD, ADHD, and/or a myriad of other mental dysfunctions and/or conditions. It is especially powerful in these cases if all the underlying and foundational childhood events can be accessed and resolved through remembering and re-member-ing, allowing true healing to occur.

Alternatively, if one truly believes in the timelessness of God and the power of love we can simply love our wounded child and ourselves back into wholeness and wellness by expressing our true nature as love rather than by experiencing ourselves as the unresolved inner conflict.

I have experienced a form of ADD (Attention Deficit Disorder) through most of my life. I have always thought this was due to a genetic predisposition, as it is inherent throughout my whole family.

And I have been aware of varying layers of anger in my psyche for many years. However, it was not until I had to deal with my prostate cancer that I was able to drill deep enough into the core source of the anger in order to identify it and resolve it. I discovered the never, ever declaration and chose to stop blaming my mother for verbally abusing me as a small child. That is what healed the cancer; simply letting go of the blame towards my mother.

Some time later that I began to become aware of the emotional chains that seemed to be sabotaging the other areas of my life including my business success and my relationships. That is when I discovered my core guilt associated with the must-be-so abandonment experience, and the forever moment that was stamped upon it. So even in blaming my mother I was also at the same time blaming myself for being guilty in some way, and worthy of abandonment.

Simply in remembering and re-member-ing that event with my adult maturity and showering my wounded child with love, I was able to resolve and dissipate my feelings of guilt and impending abandonment. And remarkably, all aspects and remnants of my former ADD condition seem to have miraculously disappeared.

I believe that these unresolved childhood conflicts not only create a predisposition for emotional trauma and disease later in life, but also lay the framework for all and asunder various forms of mental illness.

Is anyone listening?

There's more. Immediately upon finally resolving the last remnants of the abandonment 'must be so' guilt trip I had laid upon myself, my tennis game improved significantly. One day I was just a decent social player, and the next day I became competitive at a higher level.

This is the key for slipping into 'the zone' in sports. The zone is that special state of being wherein we can be and play like gods.

It would appear that some have it and some don't. I don't think that is true. I think we all have it. But most of us have way too much unresolved emotional garbage continually dragging us down with negative self belief systems based upon those early childhood experiences.

For two and a half years I have been struggling to access and hold the seventh ringing after meditation. Something always seemed to bring me 'down to earth' so to speak after my structured meditation. Suddenly, after resolving my must be so abandonment and guilt memory, I have achieved solid state being in a very high vibration. There is nothing holding me back, or dragging me back, anymore.

Those unresolved issues even affected the way I used to think. In some way, my repressed victim mentality took the line that I didn't have to do or complete 'the work,' whatever that was; that someone else had to step in to finish things off. This often resulted in shoddy or incomplete workmanship that often needed to be corrected or redone by someone else.

Suddenly, I have become naturally thorough and fastidious. Never before have I experienced those traits. I've even begun keeping a diary and maintaining it regularly. What exactly is going on here?

After trying and failing to learn how to play the guitar for years on end, I recently borrowed a guitar from a friend and found the fingering on the frets, all of a sudden, to be easily understandable and learnable. I am now, after only four hours of tinkering, playing the guitar as never before. This amounts to an entirely new way learning and thinking.

There is a hugely important lesson to be found in these experiences. It just may be that all learning deficiencies, all mental illness, all emotional dysfunctions and all serious disease finds its pre-dispositional source in our unresolved childhood trauma memories.

Think of the amazing opportunity we have of helping our children unlock and resolve their own karmic lessons before those trauma memories become buried beneath an avalanche of adult experiences added to and confusing the memory base.

This might well be the answer towards fast forwarding the spiritual evolution of mankind, and by speeding up the karmic learning of our children, beginning to end the senseless slaughter of our brothers and sisters across the world through violence and warfare.

What if we could through love release the wild genius within each of us that is desperately attempting to find its place in freedom and understanding?

Finding that genius is what life is about…and it's always been silently - and not so silently - waiting within.

THE WILDNESS

I came here to discover who I was, to find my place.

Was I the comforter? No, I did not always bring comfort.
Comfort was in me, and in you, but I was not the comforter.

Was I the peacemaker? No, I did not always bring peace.
Peace was in me, and in you, but I was not the peacemaker.

Then I felt a murmuring, a stirring in my soul; and a stirring into yours.
A wildness in me, calling out to the wildness in you.
I came to stir souls, to call them out into the wild place, the place of freedom.
The place where souls can run and dance and rejoice in nakedness and beauty.

I am the wildness, the lone wolf; calling from the mountain.
Calling, and listening.

I am the wild place; the ocean, calling home the mountain.
Calling, and waiting.

There is no comfort, but a momentary comfort.
There is no peace, but a momentary peace.
There is no rest, neither in the wolf, the mountain, nor the ocean.

Only this restlessness, this eternal stirring, calling me to myself.
And to myself I shall return, either in death, or by God's grace in this lifetime.

Loving our Karmic Bounty Hunters

Have you ever met someone in your life who seems intent on bringing you down, no matter what the circumstances? This may be a reincarnated soul (other you) that you have wronged in some way in a past life. Whenever this kind of circumstance arises, the divine spirit has orchestrated a situation in which both parties (you and your other self) may potentially learn a great lesson and acquire further wisdom in propelling yourselves upward, forward, and closer to your ultimate destiny as the one divine consciousness itself.

The person that is carrying the grudge, so to speak, continues to live and remain in victimhood, and needs to see beyond his or her perceived hurt before moving up the vibrational scale. And you need to accept the perfect karmic balance that is playing out in this relationship without defensively resisting the karmic buy-off that presents itself.

The first and most important step is to accept that everything that you have experienced in life (including all past lives) has arisen as a result of your own choices. Some persons call this the Law of Cause and Effect. Others refer to this manifestation as the Law of Attraction by which we attract into our life exactly what we express and/or expect, either from a position of guilt and low self worth, or innocence and self value.

Everything in the future follows the choices and judgments we make about ourselves now. We can either resist 'paying' a karmic debt, or meet it with compassion and understanding. And when we show up to face our karmic debts, we are released to experience our real true worth.

This is what the Biblical Jesus meant when he counseled us to 'turn the other cheek' when we meet with abuse from a supposed enemy. There are no enemies, only confused and forgetful other manifestations of our same divine self seeking some sort of spiritual justice; just as *we* are. In this case, the only real justice comes about not through punishment, but through understanding.

This is not to say that we need prostrate ourselves before our enemies, and to succumb to all their demands. This does nothing for us and nothing for them. What is important is to not fall into the temptation of trying to justify yourself, trying to be right, or trying to make them wrong. Whatever did or did not happen in the past doesn't matter. What matters is that this other person is experiencing some very real feelings that cannot easily be negotiated away. The only defense in such a situation- and it is the only defense in any situation- is to express yourself truly and purely as the love that you are.

In the final analysis, what every person needs, yearns for, and looks for in life is to be heard and understood, and to be seen and appreciated for the wonderful magic act that they are. To love your enemy is the single most potent and disarming thing you can possibly do to/for them. And in the face of such love, each of you ultimately becomes powerless to express anything other than love.

It might well be that the single act of experiencing love in this way will open that other person to embracing their own karmic expression, accepting their present circumstance (along with their past experiences) as a perfect balance, and appreciating you no longer as a villain or abuser, but rather as a person now respected and loved.

These are the circumstances that spirit brings into play as a way for us to test and measure ourselves against our own spiritual growth. If we choose to resist our karma, what is it that obviously remains unresolved in our life?

If we resist a karmic attack now, what will prevent a continuous flow of similar karmic attacks that will probably go on indefinitely until we finally resolve our karma and acquire the wisdom waiting therein?

The sooner we simply show up and face the music the sooner we grow up and move closer to who we came into life to be and experience in true magnificence.

Love takes root where nothing else will grow, even in the midst of hatred.

I LOVE, THEREFORE I AM

I've often heard it said to me,
'I think therefore I surely be.'
But I don't think that is the way
To know myself from day to day.

We think therefore we claim we are.
I say there is a higher bar.
Beyond all thought within my mind,
In silence my real self I find.

I only think because I'm not
Quite happy with what I have got.
'Cause when I think I cannot see
The truth in what's in front of me.

I see what happened yesterday;
To see the truth that's not the way.
To find and refine inner health
I've got to journey into self.

I see much more than what I've done;
'Tis then I know my life's begun.
I hear the silence there within;
And only then I know I've been.

In silence God can speak to me,
And that's when I begin to see.
God's voice makes all my thoughts go dim,
And in God's love I surely am.

Part 3:
Beyond Time & Space

From Where did We Come?

Did we choose to proceed on this journey from supposed 'everything' to our earthly experience of aloneness and separation? And if so, what was the 'we' that did the choosing? Are we truly an individual spirit body that has in the past experienced numerous other lives? Or are there an infinite number of past life experiences upon which we can choose to build our experience and our wisdom?

Given the various anecdotal accounts of persons reliving or exactly remembering places and events from remote history, often when under hypnosis, and those describing beautiful near death experiences, I tend to believe that we are truly ageless and eternal beings. Whether we remain individually and spiritually unique through the ages, or always return to the one great self between interchanges, remains an open question.

Perhaps our individual spirit identity lingers on for awhile as we contemplate the lessons and entertainment gleaned from within our earthly life. Perhaps we linger on while those near and dear to us in life continue on the earth plane. Perhaps we linger on until we can, either through contemplation, observation or earthly assistance resolve the emotional traumas that have eluded us. And perhaps we linger on because *we can;* by virtue of the lessons we have learned, the wisdom we have gained, and the understandings we have merged with our very being.

Spiritual intercession, the concept of deceased spirits contributing in some way to the lives of the living, would seem to be a relatively popular past time for those deceased souls with unfinished business, or an in-completed game, as it were. And it may well be entertaining and rewarding for enlightened souls to remain in a connected sort of spirit form as angels and emissaries between the earthly and ethereal realms.

Even Christianity, in its present orthodox form, accepts the existence of a spirit and angel realm. Its premise is founded on the eternal and undying nature of Jesus of Nazareth, and his communication with the spirit world. And even though said Jesus expounded his disciples to follow his teachings and 'do these works and more,' the modern church continues to consider spiritualists and those who heal without the blessings of Jesus to be of the 'devil,' apparently some lesser deity who exists outside of the Alpha and Omega of the Christian God.

Surely, if the God of creation is not complete within itself, embracing all of its creation; and has created a separate alter ego of sorts just to tempt, confuse, and condemn us mere mortals to eternal hell, allegiance to that sort of partial God does not appeal to me.

I prefer to believe that my God is complete, a God of infinite and unconditional love, that all things have a purpose and a reason, and that what we perceive as being imperfect or broken in life are simply manifestations of a divine disorder within which you and I can experience our true higher selves as divine order bringers. After all, even a simple card game of solitaire means nothing until the cards are shuffled again into disorder. And we are playing a much more complicated, challenging, and rewarding game; and one that pays incredible dividends in the winning.

There is a wonderful duality to life by which all things are experienced against the mirror of their exact opposites. Thus, we must have good and bad, light and darkness, happiness and anger, love and hatred, sound and silence, joy and sadness, and forgetting and remembering. So it is, the experience of the one defines the other; and we, who have the power to orchestrate the direction of our own life can choose the one or the other as our wisdom, our appetite, and our understanding permit. This reflects our karmic journey of learning.

Even by simple observation, the human world is beset with cruelty, violence, sadness, unfairness and poverty-consciousness. Humans are set against beasts, and humans are set against humans. Judging from the various religions vying for 'most sacred' status amongst the gods, humanity seems eternally set against God. Or at least one man's God is set against another man's God.

On the face of it, the world seems broken; at least in terms of humankind. It's confusing. It seems as if life is a very complex and complicated riddle that defies resolution. And this same sense of irresoluble problems pervades our personal lives as well as manifesting in the world which we create around us.

Where do we begin in sorting out the world?

Where do we begin in sorting out our own country? Where do we begin in sorting out our own community?

Where do we begin in sorting out our own family?

Where do we begin in sorting out our own relationships?

Clearly, it all begins with us. In the beginning, this is the only place where we have any power. And even though it may not feel like it, once we realize our own power, it becomes absolute as a way of choosing and creating our own unique experiences of life.

Ultimately, we can learn to choose our feelings, choose our responses, choose to love unconditionally, and open ourselves to the infinite and eternal love of the almighty that is constantly raining down on us all the time.

The world that we know is a world of illusion and lies. Since our birth, we have experienced that in a million ways. And still we hold on to so many belief systems built upon supposition, theory, culture, conspiracy, legend, outright lies, and controlling agendas, that we have no real place to stand. And not the least of these lies is the belief that we are powerless against our circumstances.

Maybe the most helpful place to start would be to get a little understanding about *what must be* rather than engage in any of the fairy tales that abound which *cannot possibly be*. In order to fully engage with life, we first must come to terms with our own aloneness, and, our own completeness within that aloneness.

Once we accept that we are alone in our circumstances, we can embrace the 'oneness' of our spiritual reality.

The infinite mind does not rule by decree. It considers it must be so – and for a reason. Therefore it is.

A SINGLE SOUL

I am a single soul. A soul alone, I'm free to search for self.
The key I've found within to open others; my true wealth.

In taking risks in life and love, in standing out my old beliefs, and painful past;
What comes may come, but to the precious moment I hold fast.

No compromise to stand my truth and journey ever on.
No peace to keep in other's home, no beliefs laid out like bear traps covered slight
upon.

No dead and loathsome baggage, compromises asked;
No obstacles to climb, which can't be met as task.

I am at peace, I own my time, accept my illness and my health.
I live for me, I am my work; I am a story writes itself.

I see the world just as it is. I meet my world at quickening pace.
No winners picked, no rules embrace; I choose the journey, not the race.

Sometimes, I stop to breathe and dress my wound.
Sweet wound it be, that dresses me, that gives me further sight and sound.

Priceless wounds by which I've blazed along the trail my journey there to here.
Perhaps, because my trail, another comes this way and feels less fear.

I've come from out a wooded place with shadows, hidden nooks, and sheltered view.
A place to hide and shed my skin beneath a rock, to come anew.
Or change my spots, just like a fawn who lived in shade, then finally grew.

It seems a peaceful meadow stretches now before.
In light and openness, I look afar and see much more.
This be my new domain; just like the stag, I sound my roar!

New self, new self! I do declare to meadow and to glade!
I'm not the past! I'm so much more, I've been remade.

Bliss falls upon my face when ere I look where light and life begin.
A glorious place to be and journey through, and if must be, to end.

The price we pay for seeing further, standing taller;
Targets we then be for others, those men smaller.

Now I know my way; and others, too, may join me here, and stay.
Perhaps my blaze and roar will be a calling; them, who chance to come this way.

I choose it so.   This meadow has a place for every fragrant flower.
All beings, come, that bless the sunshine; also, that which brings the shower.

In joy stand I to count them every one, and honor, too, their paths, which echo none.
In love and truth we simply join; our separate paths towards one great sum.

And as each flower blesses me with fragrance dancing 'cross the field,
I bless them, too, with all I am; there's nothing here to give, but all to yield.

But if there were a gift to give, I hope that you would pleasure self to see,
What ere I had, or got from some, the trophy of my life, I would surrender up to
thee.

What's it All About?

If there is such a thing as a divine, infinite, and everlasting intelligence, let's assume that it has some degree of common sense; at least on a par with our own. Now, if you were this divine essence, being all that there was, what would there be outside of yourself that you could experience? Being everything totally removes the possibility of experiencing anything outside of yourself.

In our human bodies, all our senses are designed to register and experience phenomena occurring outside of ourselves that interface with us in some way. We relate to our environment from a position of being separate from it. The very act of experiencing requires us to be separate from that which we experience. Thus, to be everything (as in being God) is to experience nothing. At least from the human mind perspective, being God creates an experiential impossibility.

So here you are, the great something-ness floating around in a great nothing-ness, with nothing to see, nothing to hear, nothing to touch, nothing to feel, nothing to taste, nothing to smell, and nothing, outside of yourself, to experience in any way. Infinite and eternal boredom then takes on a whole new meaning.

Luckily for ourselves, the divine essence seems to have a few tricks up its sleeves. It knows how to make and to use magic. It knows how to divide itself, and multiply itself. It knows how to add to itself and subtract from itself. It knows mathematics, quantum physics, science, and biology. In fact, it created all of those. It knows how to create something from nothing. It knows everything; the past, the present and the future combined! Importantly it knows how to forget.

And therein lies the real magic. In forgetting everything, the great I AM sets the stage for experiencing something. A smorgasbord of somethings.

You and I are the vehicles through which this great forgetfulness manifests. We are born into forgetfulness, believing ourselves to be separate from the cosmos at birth. And from that humble beginning of utter helplessness, meaninglessness, forgetfulness, and separation begins our noble journey through life in quest of remembering, meaning, and at least a partial reconnection to the great self.

The whole meaning of life lies in the very experience of connecting; connecting with oneself, connecting with others and re-connecting with the great I AM; that which we all are at our source. In reconnecting we find ourselves intimately immersed in both the infinitesimal and infinite perfection of all things.

Our struggles are a patient curiosity to the great I AM until we recognize the game and learn the rules…

God is ecstatic when we finally join his team in the game.

The Universal Identity Crisis

We all come into life in order to face, and to resolve, a grand cosmic identity crisis. Only in experiencing complete separation from our true selves can we then begin the long journey back towards remembering, in *part*, who we really are. The magic word here is part.

Our challenge as spiritual alchemists is to retain enough of our imperfections and flaws to ensure we can look upon God without being absorbed back into the great something-nothing wherein there is no experience to be had. The perfect duality exists when we can watch God from a distance and God can watch us from a distance; each of us experiencing in duality what neither can experience without the other.

Because in remembering fully who and what we are, we would become the final whole and lose access to the magic of the parts. There can be no ending in God, because we would simply disappear within the great all. And in a very true sense there is no finality to anything; except perhaps the perceived finality of our karmic forever moments that only needed to be resolved in order to move us on in our eternal journey towards bliss.

Thus, the more intensely we embrace our circumstances as our identity, the ever more surely the divine hand of karma will present us with the very change in circumstances that will force us to reevaluate our belief systems and take another step away from our victimhood and towards our imminent partial godhood, allowing us to experience ourselves within God as well as beside him.

Free choice is the basis for all experience. The God within us is helping us choose, through our karmic lessons, a state of existence or experiencing that is so close to enfolding us in the all-ness of God that a single step inward would lead to complete reunion with the great self, and, the cessation of all outward feelings or experiences. We seek to become illumined angels, maintaining only the infinitesimal element of ego necessary to separate us sufficiently from the great self so that we can experience the perfect beauty, magic, and mystery of God and its creations all around us. To be in such a state is to be in eternal bliss, forever praising the perfect love of God, who is also experiencing bliss through us.

As humans we can experience this ourselves, as angels do. This is, in fact, our destiny. We are here learning to be angels, or at least angelic beings. By standing within and becoming the seven mystic vibrations of creation, we experience the bliss of the mind of God. This can occur for a moment or a lifetime, as the mind of God is always with us, waiting for us to partner with it.

By allowing our soul to shine forth and rejoin with the soul of God in another person, we see the divine beauty of God in reflection. This can be a continuous experience with a single person and/or occurring with many different persons as we meet them passing through life.

And in the sacred touching of another person's heart, which is the heart of God, we can, through Tantric oneness hang indefinitely within the exquisite feeling of love which emits from out the Heart of God. The magic of love making is not in fact the orgasm.

The doorway to God significantly closes at orgasm. The most amazing heart connection with God occurs at that place just before orgasm. It is possible to stand there for an indefinite time experiencing the exquisite feelings of love as two hearts merge as one; and indeed prolong that moment repeatedly again and again for an evening, or for a lifetime.

Our challenge, and our opportunity, is to hold back from the need to find finality in life, and to learn to appreciate the eternal flow of love as it continually passes through us. As we allow ourselves to be worthy of God's love, we will gradually grow closer and closer to him in praise, gratitude, and an ever deepening respect.

This is precisely what our destiny as angels has in store for us. To stand so close to God in his glory, that we are continually bathed in his blissful love without ever having to disappear into finality or cosmic nothingness.

So long as we seek out the finalities of orgasm, success, and victory in life we lose access to the most wonderful gift of all, an eternal life in bliss. Our need for finality will always return us to the karmic wheel of life until we surrender to love on its own terms, accept bliss as a continual flowing through of love, and abandon our need to find momentary completion whether in physicality, sexuality, relationship, business, family or friendship.

Life extends only so far in front of us as we can reach out and touch with our hand. Infinity and eternity are both embraced in our own single moment. Our moment flows as light through an open door. Close not, however bright.

The eyes, mind, and heart adjust to bliss with passing time.

The Magic Shift in Near-Death Experiences

Many persons who have come close to death report a near death experience that profoundly changes their perspective and experience of life.

Often they find themselves outside of their body observing the frantic attempts by doctors to resuscitate the patient, who has obviously begun to exhibit the classic medical signs of death. That is, the cessation of breathing and heartbeat.

Anita Moorjani was in the last stages of dying from cancer when she fell into a long coma. While in the coma, she left her body and experienced the bliss of God's unconditional love. Finally choosing to return to her body, she knew that she would be healed, and she was. Her experience changed her perspective and her life. She now travels and speaks extensively about her experience, now also described in her book, *Dying to Be Me*.

For most, the *Near Death* phenomenon becomes an exquisite experience of bliss, and the feeling of being held in unconditional love. Many long to continue towards the waiting 'light' within which they are basking, and only reluctantly agree to return to within their body which holds and represents their earthly circumstances.

Those persons almost without exception bring back with them a totally new perspective on life and on what they are. They have discovered and experienced their 'real' self which is an ageless and eternal spirit entity which we may as well call the soul. They no longer fear death, and generally begin to restructure their lives around family, friends, and loved ones rather than the normal pursuits of financial or commercial success.

In essence, what has happened to them is that they have been gifted the opportunity to view themselves through the eyes of their own eternal higher selves. This is exactly the shift in perspective that is necessary for us to take on in our lives in order to rise above our circumstances, whatever they may be, and become the masters of our own lives.

In observing our circumstances, we become master over them. In observing our pain, we rise above it. In observing our emotions, we become separate from them and can choose our own emotional responses. In observing the wounded child crying out from within, we 'become' the hand of God reaching out to comfort, nurture, and heal that child, fulfilling his or her needs exactly as required.

As the child heals, we are healed. Our chains fall away whether they are the chains of original sin or simply the unresolved chains of karmic learning. In letting go of what we are not, we automatically inherit a new sense of what we are; an ageless and eternal spiritual being on a journey from pain to pleasure, from loneliness to connection, and from unhappiness to bliss.

We arrive at love. That love, which in forgetfulness, we have always been.

My Near-Death Experience

Years ago when I was just a young child a wonderful man came into my life. His name was Rod Alderton, a traveling representative of the Oldsmobile automotive manufacturing company. He regularly called on my father's auto dealership, and invariably stayed overnight with my family. For many years he came into and out of our lives, always spending time with my brothers and me, and teaching us all the finer points of billiards, among other things. All my siblings loved Rod. In a way he was like a second father to me.

Eventually Rod declared that he would wait for my sister Janice, who was ten years his junior, to grow up before he married. And that is what he did.

Rod was over two meters tall and had a heart to match. They married some time around 1958 after sister Jan had given birth to another man's child out of wedlock. The two of them then jumped through some very difficult hoops in order to reclaim the birth child and adopt her.

After reluctantly moving to Storm Lake, Iowa, to assist Dad in his auto dealership, around 1970 Rod contracted cancer and underwent intensive and invasive treatment, which seemed to cure him. Then for a few years he was groomed by Dad to take over the Peterson automotive sales business. By this time he and sister Jan were pretty well wrapped up in their life. Sadly, after the first child was born out of wedlock, Jan was unable to conceive again. They went on to adopt another eight children from broken or abusive homes; perhaps in a spirit of atonement.

I went AWOL to Canada in 1968, spent two years in the Sideras commune ending in 1971, and then three years creating a financial nest egg in Nova Scotia, Canada, before finding and settling on my remote property in Fiji in 1974. While in Fiji I continued to build upon my spiritual journey began in earnest in the commune, and often wished I could share some of that journey with my beloved brother-in-law Rod. It was not to be in the physical sense.

My father died in 1977, and Rod was there to step in and mind the business.

At this time I was living on my remote five hundred acres in Fiji and making a three-day trip to Labasa town each week in order to sell produce and buy provisions. Lettie Chute was a good friend living in Labasa who provided accommodation for my family and myself whenever we needed to be overnight in Labasa.

I arrived at Lettie's home late one evening, shared a meal with Lettie and then went right to bed. For some reason I was unable to fall asleep. Even my meditation failed me. For hours I struggled with myself in consternation and confusion.

Late into the night a pain began to develop in my chest. The pain became unbearable. Finally, my lungs became paralyzed and I could not take a breath.

I called out to God in my own way. *Father, what is happening to me?*

God replied, *I'm calling you home.*

I can't go now. I must look after my family. They have no one else.

Don't worry. They have a God, too.

I heard it, and I finally got it. I surrendered myself, in trust, to God's will. I accepted my death and put my destiny – and the destiny of my family - in God's hands.

Instantly, all the pain left me and I was filled with ecstasy and bliss. For a few minutes I lay there in awe and gratitude. Although I was not dead, I was somehow somewhere above life. And if this was life, it was life as I had never known it. I was somehow connected to all things, experiencing the entire community – even the whole world - around me as a living, breathing organism in itself.

I was being held in God's love, desiring nothing else but for that love to continue. For certain, I had no more regrets or apprehensions about dying. If this was death, let me have more of it.

Suddenly and without warning something came out of the darkness, thumped me squarely in the pit of my stomach and crashed onto the floor. It was a silver crucifix that had been resting on a high shelf several feet away from the bed. Some kind of higher power had intervened and upended the law of gravity, perhaps using this media to bring home a message of some sort. What was the message?

For the rest of the night I lay awake in a state of heightened awareness and wonder. The next morning after sharing my experience with Lettie, a devout Catholic who was certain that all would be revealed, I made my six-monthly phone call back to my mother and siblings in Iowa, USA. My sister Jan answered the phone.

How did you know? We didn't know how to contact you.

Know what?

Rod died twelve hours ago. From pneumonia.

That was all she could manage to say before breaking down into sobbing incoherence.

Pneumonia. The lungs fill with liquid and become paralyzed. It's a painful way to die. I know the pain of it.

Somehow across ten thousand miles I was able to take Rod's hand and cross the veil with him into the next life; and was indeed able to give back to him some of the love he had shared with me. Rod had made a difference to me and I to him. That experience changed both of our lives. I have never again been afraid of death or afraid of life.

Perhaps I had helped Rod learn how to die with grace, and he had, as before, taught me how to *live* with grace.

The Science behind my Reality

Quantum physicists are beginning to understand that the particles of matter are not necessarily matter at all. All this supposed matter is actually energy in motion. To simplify things, science calls this matter 'light'; electrons, neutrons, protons, quirks, quarks and numerous other little fellows doing their thing in a particular manner manifesting as one thing or another.

Strangely, science has not quite been able to nail down just what this 'light' stuff is. One minute it manifests as a measurable particle. The next minute (or the same minute) it appears as a wave or vibration of some sort. This follows Einstein's view that matter and energy are both indestructible and interchangeable. This also follows the religious view that the essence of all creation- God, if you will - is both ageless and eternal. It also follows that if the substance of all things is simply a vibration or wave of energy, it is the varying vibrations that distinguish one thing from another, one person from another, and one time from another. Science calls this field of energy that manifests either as waves or particles the Quantum Hologram.

When we are lost within the hologram we seem to be absolutely subject to it. Once we begin to realize that we *are* the hologram experiencing it from the inside out through our own unique perspective, everything begins to change. The circumstances of time and space lose their hold on us as we begin to experience our infinite and eternal nature. Nutrition becomes less significant as we learn to accept and absorb the divine vibrations - prana - as the real source of our substance. And our need for action and 'doing' gives way to an appreciation of pure being.

Through conscious choice, we embellish the Quantum Hologram with every thought, word and action.

...for us physicists believe the separation between past, present, and future is only an illusion, although a convincing one.

Albert Einstein

THE QUANTUM HOLOGRAM

There is a way of seeing through a hole in time and space.
Where all things are that ever were; the future, too, in place.
Of seeing things a long way off, as through a mystic lens,
Of understanding why we 'did,' our guilt, through knowledge, cleanse.

A place of clarity and ease that transcends earthly worry.
A place where time does not exist; and so, no need to hurry.
This is the Quantum Hologram where we and God combine.
In partnership we share our roles, each other to define.

We must pretend to stand apart, in pieces find our wealth.
If we were what we looked upon, how could we see ourself?
We must remember always that we only are a part.
There is no final end to reach, we can but choose to start.

There is no place we're going to that takes us out of now.
It's not a case of going where but rather going how.
The Quantum Hologram exists for those who dare to feel.
For those who choose to guard their heart, it all must seem unreal.

And so it is for those that choose to live within their past,
From old experiences they hold, the future is then cast.
It all exists within the Quantum Hologram, you see.
There is no right or wrong, we simply choose what we will be.

To life we must surrender, that's how we learn to grow.
Our spirit wants to move ahead, if we just let it go.
We can behave like animals if that appeals to us,
But if we do we just might find that we have missed the bus.

When we connect with our great self, there is so much to know.
The how, the why, the when and the which way we should then go.
Life then becomes much easier, for us to smell the flowers,
And from the Quantum Hologram we're gifted awesome powers.

Within the Quantum Hologram it seems we are held fast.
But with our own mortality, it seems it cannot last.
We're simply here to know ourselves from inside out, you see.
That's how God entertains itself and why we came to be.

Manifesting the Universe

Generally speaking, there is a hierarchy of vibration that we can observe within the Quantum Hologram.

There are various observable forms of energy. There is a whole spectrum (vibration) of light, some perceivable to the human eye, and much not. Likewise, there is sound; again only a limited range that we can perceive. We also know about electricity, magnetism, gravity, and two distinct types of energy holding atomic structure together. At these levels of vibration, there is no separation. The pure vibration of creation can be equated with the Word: 'In the beginning was the Word.'

When these various vibrations reach a certain threshold, they begin to manifest in a solid state. Matter is born, and thus the heavens and the firmament take shape, following a divine order.

Water is the birthplace of life; and water itself strangely takes on life-like properties that defy scientific explanation. The making of the lakes, rivers, oceans, and water in the atmosphere requires its own unique vibration of creation, a higher Word of God.

As the land was watered by the rain from the heavens, fed by the minerals of the land, and blessed by the alchemy of the sun's rays, algae, fungus, and plant life emerged on the earth, displaying a new, higher vibration; and a unique new type of consciousness, or self awareness.

Another new vibration then begat the emergence of single-celled organisms in the seas, ultimately leading towards fishes and all manners of marine organisms.

The next vibration of creation led to the development of birds and reptiles, increasingly becoming more and more conscious of their own consciousness.

Finally, a higher vibration brought forth the animals and creatures of the land, of which man is one. To this point, all the vibrations and their subsets hold as an ultimate truth a vibration of pure being. Even man holds that potential within himself. This is akin to a deck of cards all being prearranged so that the proverbial game of solitaire always proceeds in a way in which the player always wins.

The seventh vibration brought a new element into the game; the opportunity for humans *not to be*. Ultimately, humankind became conscious of itself as a decision maker, the creative element embodied within the new ability *not to be*. God, through humankind, was finally able to forget itself in order to create an entirely new existence of experience. With his ability to choose *not to be*, he also gained the ability to access an incredible higher 'beingness' while in physical form, an entirely new appreciation of all the positive emotions held in freedom, the ability to choose his own vibrations, and therefore the ability to choose the quality of his experiences.

The Bible, in Genesis, speaks of the world being created in six days, with God resting on the seventh. Metaphorically speaking, this might equate to the seven general vibrations of creation beginning with the pure non-experiential primal vibration (word) of God before creation (if there was such a state), and culminating in the human capacity to achieve divine creative 'beingness' while still in human form. Some would call this elevated state enlightenment. The small 'me' would call this state 'resting in the mind, heart, and soul of God.' The God in me might call it resting in the mind, heart, and soul of Man.

Clearly, there is a whole range of human possibility ranging from animalistic and barbaric behavior, and through various ascending levels of grace before reaching that ultimate place of divine connection spoken of by few, and experienced by fewer still.

By experiencing the seven vibrations as manifested in the seven ringings of stillness, or their equivalent in clairvoyance and clairsentience, mankind gains access to all the wisdom, knowledge, and magic held within all creation; and ultimately achieves the ability to create, consciously experience, and 'be' simultaneously. And thus God has created the ultimate infinite and eternal entertainment centre for itself.

Ultimately, the god in me has chosen that I will succeed in my journey of entertainment and enlightenment. I have placed challenges before myself that ensure that, sooner or later, I will surmount those challenges and win the prizes held there within.

Not only have I chosen a creation that is constantly in a state of movement and change, it is constantly destroying and renewing itself in a never-ending dance of life, death and renewal. For my own entertainment and enjoyment, the deck is being constantly reshuffled.

UNCONDITIONAL LIFE

The grass, stretching up from the warm, moist soil, dances in the wind with the buffalo. When its hour is come it gives itself up to the buffalo.
In that moment both are joined in the love of life, and are transformed.
The grass becomes the buffalo.
Unconditional life. Life feasting upon itself.

The buffalo, searching out the succulent grasses, dances with the Plains Indian.
When its hour is come, it gives itself up to the Indian.
In that moment, both are joined in the love of life, and are transformed.
The buffalo becomes the Plains Indian.
Unconditional life. Life feasting upon itself.

The Plains Indian, hunting out the sustenance of the buffalo, dances with life itself; the seasons, the famines, the droughts ~ each demanding a different dance.
When his hour is come he gives himself up to life and is transformed; loving life even more in its transformation than in its first coming.
Unconditional life. Life feasting upon itself.

The wildebeest pauses for the succulent grasses and sweet tastes of the watering hole, and dances with the lion.
When its hour is come it gives itself up to the lion.
In that moment both are joined in the love of life and are transformed.
Unconditional life. Life feasting upon itself.

The lion exalts in its success; the wildebeest clinging to life
even as the lion gorges on its entrails.
Unconditional life. Life feasting upon itself.

The lion searches and waits for the tiring wildebeest, and dances with its
own hunger and age.
When its hour is come, it gives itself up to the vulture and the hyena.
In that moment, all are joined in the love of life and are transformed.
The lion becomes the vulture and the hyena.
Unconditional life. Life feasting upon itself.

The caribou follows the seasons, seeking out the new growth and the old,
and dances with the wolf.
When its hour is come, it gives itself up to the wolf.
In that moment both are rejoined in the love of life, and are transformed.
The caribou becomes the wolf.
Unconditional life. Life feasting upon itself.

The wolf follows the caribou unceasingly, dancing with its own hunger.
When its hour is come, it gives itself up to the seasons and the grasses.
All are joined in the love of life, and are transformed.
The wolf becomes the seasons, and the grasses.
Unconditional life. Life feasting upon itself.

Who am I to break the dance of life and call for rest before the final note
resounds?
Have I not eyes to see the way that life in truth and brutal love rebounds?

Need I tread softly in my dance, and watch while idle time devours the
rhythm of my life?
Or should I nip your heels within the chase, and cause you anger/passion
with to rise above your strife?

I came to dance, and teach the dance; call others to the ballroom floor.
To lead, perhaps, or to be led, through yet another awesome door.

It matters not just where we go, the game is neither lost nor won.
The dancers, in their own sweet time, retire 'fore the next song sung.

Again life feasts upon itself; one cycle ended, one begun.
They play our song, the dance is now, before the midnight hour is rung.

The Cause of all Illnesses?

I now believe that most or all illness is caused by the retention in our mind/body/soul field of unresolved emotional traumas. These traumas almost certainly settle upon us at the moment of our birth when we have been thrust out from a safe and comfortable environment into a new and seemingly hostile one.

It is likely that all our unresolved karmic lessons from past lives are bundled up into a package meant just for us, and delivered to us directly during that birth. Thus, we cannot escape our karma, no matter how hard we might try. It may be that there is a sort of chord or chords stretching from the karmic foundational events of the past (instances wherein we were the abuser) through to our own child selves, and then forever forward in life with us from our child selves until they are resolved.

For many, the pain is simply too great to accept and own as our very own. Thus we spend most if not all of our life running away from the pain and the karmic lessons being carried by it. When we do that, we are actually running away from our own injured and hurting child self, whom we have left to carry the burden of our own unresolved lessons.

Difficult and as uncomfortable as it might have been, because we had no intellectual or emotional means to define our birthing experience, initially we had no choice but to sit with it and be with it (our helplessness) for a while until we could begin to make some sense of our surroundings.

After a time we began to define our feelings, and it is at this time that we probably recorded our first memorable abandonment and anger experiences. It is upon these very early experiences that our karmic lessons attach themselves. They may come from past lives, a new karmic lesson from the immediately preceding life, or unresolved ancestral issues connecting to us through our blood line.

From wherever they have come, they are ours and ours alone to resolve; and they will keep connecting with us throughout this life and the next unless and until we have the courage to accept, embrace and own them.

The unresolved karmic content naturally triggers our own peculiar emotional responses, and explains why different individuals respond quite differently to the same events, or types of events. One event, unrelated to any karmic lesson, may be experienced simply as a short uncomfortable learning experience by one person. The same event, imbued with a karmic lesson, may be a traumatic experience for another person.

In fact, it just may be that all illness manifests as a perfect expression of a person's karmic journey through life representing an important lesson that person has till then failed to honor and/or resolve. Inevitably, the longer a person refuses to accept the lesson, the more serious the physical or mental effect upon us becomes.

We tire under a heavy burden. Maybe it's time to set it down.

The Hamer Postulate

These karmic-laden trauma events also seem to affect different parts of the brain designed to deal with particular types of archetypal challenges experienced in our evolutionary past.

In our development through the ages as an ever more conscious human entity, we have continually preserved the automatic animalistic behaviors developed to cope with environmental challenges occurring before this new form of consciousness arose. These are the classic fight, flee, or freeze responses which can be observed in most forms of animal, reptile, fish or bird life.

Such responses are thought to be held within the 'reptilian' old brain that we seem to hold in common with many other species of animals, reptiles, birds, and fishes.

While in fetus, our brains developed in perfect conjunction with specific organs of the body. One part of the brain develops along with the heart, for example. Another, along with the lungs. Another, the liver. Then the kidneys, etc.

Those connective roots were important during the 'start up' phase of our life, and they continue to be important throughout our later life. It would seem that the brain evolved the abilities to cope with and handle ever more complex emotional circumstances in perfect sync with the development of specific organs, or organ systems.

Thus, different types of trauma events would be met and dealt with by different parts of the human brain.

It follows, then, that unresolved trauma (largely karmically instigated) events that lodge in a certain part of the brain might easily create a 'follow on' type of event affecting specific organs.

A Dr. Hamer from Germany has developed a very specific cosmology that seems to prove this very thesis.

Dr. Hamer studied and reviewed more than 30,000 individual cases of disease and life-threatening cancers, and found that an unexpected trauma shock leaves an identifiable lesion on a particular part of the brain assigned that part of emotional trauma resolution.

Even more interestingly, the identified lesion almost always manifests in conjunction with a metabolistic change in the companion organ or organs. This often leads to serious illness and even death, often as a result of malfunction or cancerous growths appearing in the related organ.

Dr. Hamer calls this a 'special biological program' designed to help the physical organism deal with an immediate threat until the trauma itself can be resolved at a later time; at which time a healing, or healing crisis emerges which can be even more serious than the original event. Further information about Dr. Hamer's work, which has been vilified by mainstream medicine, can be found at the website http://www.newmedicine.ca/.

According to Dr. Hamer, complete healing can only occur once the originating trauma has been resolved. Otherwise, the effected organ never completely recovers from the fight, flee or freeze metabolistic pre-programmed response; remaining uncomfortably outside a pure healing environment.

Dr. Hamer concludes that, once the originating trauma has been identified and resolved, the body then switches into a healing mode and generally heals itself, given sufficient rest, protein, nutrition, love, and peace of mind. Unfortunately, the healing event itself may present crisis requiring careful management in order to prevent an overreaction of the body's functions; particularly if proper nutrition and a conducive environment are lacking in any substantial manner.

Dr. Hamer believes that these life-threatening diseases are a result of recent trauma events in our lives that we have a difficult time coming to terms with. It begs the question, then, of why some persons succumb to serious disease, and others 'weather the storm' with little or no collateral damage. I believe that the answer to this question is to be found somewhere back in the very early years of our life; when we began creating emotional responses and coping mechanisms in opposition to our spiritually inherited karmic lessons that then followed us through our later lives.

Of particular importance is the first three years of childhood; the period before we gained mastery over language. During that period of our lives our language was that of feelings. Understanding was a thing of the future, and feelings were all that we had to go by. We were also powerless in our circumstances; and depending upon the love, care, and understanding (or lack of) of our principal caregivers, prone to a continuing deep sense of abandonment, guilt, or worthlessness, and reluctant to express our emotions for fear of abuse and/or punishment.

So many of the emotional traumas we experienced while young were internalized rather than expressed and resolved. These unresolved emotional traumas, difficult as they are to remember in the absence of a defining language base at the time, then established a pre-disposition for later specific diseases which may occur should serious later trauma impact directly upon the unresolved childhood event(s), which themselves could very well be based upon unresolved past life issues.

This predisposition to disease and dis-ease then becomes exasperated every time some new similar event occurs in our lives. This often manifests as an overwhelming negative emotional response that we cannot quite put our finger upon, but that renews with a vengeance the original fight, flee or freeze response initiated in the original emotional childhood experience.

Or, as in the case of Dr. Hamer's studies, this pre-disposition can manifest as an adult severe shock trauma impacting directly upon the unresolved childhood issues, and sending the victim's body into an excessive spiral of metabolic dysfunction leading to cancer or other illness.

Adding on to the degree of difficulty in accessing these pre-language trauma memories is the aspect of the must be so acceptance of guilt, the forever moments of torment, and the never, ever declarations that we tend to imbue these early trauma memories with. Until we are able to remember and re-experience the must be so acceptance, the forever moments, and the never, ever declaration content of the memory, or resolve them by truly loving the child within, we will likely remain a slave to the emotional content held therein, and suffer a continuing game of tag as we try to distance ourselves from our own important and necessary karmic lessons.

There is an increasing body of evidence that the cells of our bodies hold all the memories of our life, or somehow give access to those same experiences. Dr. Deepak Chopra is a leading expert in this field of investigation. Dr. Chopra believes that in order to heal sickness and disease caused by emotional trauma, two elements need to be present.

First, the victim needs to somehow access the healing energy of his/her own higher self. This implies the acceptance of and connection with some energy source independent of and higher than our own cognitive self belief system or ego.

The second requirement is that we somehow access, remember, re-frame and/or resolve the disruptive and unresolved emotional traumas that lie held or accessible within the cells of our body. Dr. Chopra's research shows that most of the remarkable recoveries that he has studied follow this two step process.

Somehow, in continuing to carry an element of blame, either towards our self or other persons, we interfere with our own innate healing process, eventually leading to the predisposition for the later manifestation of serious disease. The work of both Brandon Bays and Deepak Chopra support the theory that unresolved childhood traumas (and the resulting deeply internalized coping strategies) create the predisposition towards development of serious illness later in life following Dr. Hamer's postulations relating adult shock traumas with serious illnesses.

The more I study and learn about the physical impact of emotional trauma, the more convinced I am that all serious illness derives from unresolved emotional trauma events, either in childhood or later in life. We may as well call this a result of our refusing to accept and embrace our karmic responsibilities; and refuse to accept the reality that everything about our circumstances has come about as a result of our own choices.

Total enlightenment assumes a complete independence from any attachment to the past, including the resolution of all remaining karmic lessons. Anything less assumes some degree of remaining attachment; and consequently the harboring of some significant remaining degree of ego or circumstantial belief system that interferes with the divine conversation.

To be pure in love, is to be pure of any attachments to the past, free of uncompleted karmic lessons, and to be pure of any polluting belief systems that might otherwise interfere with the flow of the divine healthy and perfect blueprint gifted us with our life.

The message is clear: If you want to be healthy, be love. To be love, one must release any sense of blame or victimhood in relation to others. No one else is responsible for our problems and challenges. It is we ourselves who have made our choices, and chosen our challenges.

Love is only found in the moment. And before it can be experienced, it must be found within our own selves. Being love is the only way to be truly healthy. It is also the only way to be truly happy. It is also the only way to be in true relationship. And it is the only way to have meaning and fulfillment in our lives.

How you get there doesn't matter. Some people find love in the most remote of places; often in the complete absence of any expectation. Therein lies one of the bizarre paradoxes of life. In the wanting, the needing, the hoping, and the expectation of finding love, one creates the greatest of barriers towards actually finding love.

You will never 'find' love in another place, person, or time, no matter how far you travel; no matter how many persons you meet, and no matter how many times you try. Love has never been about finding anything. It's about discovering your true self; that which you always have been and always will be. It is the place closest to home. It is the person you are always with. It is always this moment and none other. It is about climbing aboard your own personal transport vehicle in order to continue the eternal journey of self-discovery, self-worship, self-appreciation, and endless bliss.

But you've got to be in the driver's seat. You've got to be making all the calls. Otherwise you just might end up sharing in another person's hell.

You can turn your vehicle into a bus, a 747 jet or a giant ocean liner. Why not invite a few others along? Make your way, and show your way. If you're happy, your passengers will be happy. And if not, they will learn happiness, provided they stay on your bus.

No one can stand to be around happy people unless they are willing to try it on themselves. Share your way enough, and sooner or later, your way will show itself back to you; and you might, just might, see more of yourself in the person next to you than you even see in yourself. This is what real relationship is all about.

The universe experiences itself in the eyes, ears, and touch of another 'it.' You're it and I'm it, provided we simply accept our divine birthright and fate, and allow ourselves to experience life as God meant it to be. That is, to be whole and complete in the moment with no attachment to the things and experiences of the past.

I experience myself for the universe, and God loves through me and to me as I permit.

An unbreakable partnership. I provide the hardware and God provides the software.

Our Inner Child Lives in Us

Science is now beginning to understand that what we perceive as matter is actually tiny particles or waves of energy held within a great and infinite boundless space of apparent nothingness. When we examine the construct of the molecules and atoms of our bodies, we perceive that we are for the most part a great emptiness only slightly interspaced with waves or vibrations of information. It is from this great emptiness that the mind of God speaks to us, directing its divine karmic dance which is itself connected to all times, places, persons and experiences.

And so, the old unresolved emotions that keep rising up within us during our lives may not be memories at all. It is all the more likely that these events are in actuality our real and present child selves speaking directly to us from their 'now' through a window in the mind of God as surely as if there was a wormhole or time warp in space in which a person in one time and/or space can speak directly to a person in another time and/or space.

In these instances, that child self is speaking to us in feelings rather than words, because that is probably the only language he or she knew at the time. It is the dissonance created by the unresolved karmic lesson given to our child self and still held in time that leads to dis-ease, discomfort, and disease; which are themselves simply powerful invitations to resolve the unresolved, heal the wounded child still crying out for love, and move on in our spiritual journey.

Why would the perfect God- the ultimate magician and the inventor and owner of all time- entrust the all important mission of forwarding our spiritual journey through karmic learning, to the frailties of human recall- which itself is so often distorted by the subconscious cry of the wounded child within?

Why would she not, like the telephone operators of old, simply connect the real wounded child of our past to every experience of our present that might offer another opportunity for us to accept, resolve, and learn the karmic lesson waiting for us to unravel so we can then raise our consciousness to the next higher vibration in love?

In point of argument, why then could not all the unresolved karma of past lives settle in that singular karmic abandonment event of the infant child as a legion of voices flowing from our other selves that we have abused in some way in past lives?

For he said unto him, Come out of the man, thou unclean spirit. And he (Jesus) asked him, what is thy name? And he answered, saying, My name is Legion: for we are many.

Mark 5, vs.8 and 9

It may well be that only the child or those with obvious mental illness hear the discord of the many voices, but the 'normal' adult hears only the singular voice of the child reeling under the weight of a combined karmic package.

Why would it be any other way? It must be so.

That unloved child that you were quite literally lives on within you and through you now begging for the love he or she never received then. The pain you feel in your gut, or wherever it is located, is real pain, and there is a real child there begging for your help. To *believe in* and *to love* your inner child is the most awesome and amazing work you will ever do in your life. Until that work is successfully completed, you will never be whole in your relationship with another human being.

This truly is the work of God, which is to love his children as only a father can do. And you are the father to your own inner child, just as you also are a child of God. Would you love your own inner child any less than God would love you? And would God love you any less than you would love your own child? I don't think so.

The simple act of fully acknowledging and loving your own inner child will release you from your karmic lesson, even without remembering the foundational karmic event from which the 'memory' originated. The truth is there is nothing that you have been guilty of throughout life that was not simply an expression of your childish ignorance and your own unfounded sense of insignificance.

Identifying and accepting your wounded inner child as the unique living entity that he or she is releases you from the pain that child is experiencing. And the mature you of the present 'now' has the power through love to heal and transform the wounded child back to wholeness and happiness. Therefore, love your former selves in all your failures as well as your successes.

All the events of our lives are accessible to us for healing through the mind of God. Sixty years or six minutes ago, the same process applies. Whatever happened and however you felt then can be resolved and healed by love right now.

By observing the past we can become the present. It is through the present that the healing balm of love flows, and from nowhere else. Separate your observer self from your pain and you will be able to magically love your pain, and your loneliness, away. This is the ultimate form of power and freedom. This is how a man or a woman finds out who they are and establishes a kingdom of love within.

The God in me declares that you are forgiven for all your failings, and you are now released from your karmic burdens in order to play, live, and love - like the God you were born to be.

I am just a messenger. God has already forgiven you. Let it be. Let the loving begin.

As it already is and forever will be, it must be so.

Only You Can Heal Your Wounded Child

Most persons live a life of hopefulness. Hopeful that someday someone will come into their life- or some circumstance will change in such a way- that all their unresolved karmic issues will magically be lifted from upon their shoulders.

Sometimes the simplest of things in life are overlooked. The traumas that we have experienced in our life are unique to us in every way. They are ours and ours alone. No one else is involved in our personal feeling experiences.

How could anyone else truly know how we felt, why we felt or when we felt? And no one else can possibly know from where or when our personal karmic lessons originated. Consequently there is no one else that we can turn to who can really help us save ourselves.

And thus it is no great surprise that all those trauma experiences from our past continue to hunt us down and haunt us demanding- even praying- for resolution and fulfillment through us. They (our former selves) target us, because in some intuitive way they (our past selves) knew/know that there is one and only one real avenue of healing. And that lies only in the very present moment wherein we can, with proper insight, intention and direction connect directly to and with the mind of God.

It is only in this ever present 'now' that we can connect with our higher self and access the wonderful healing power of unconditional love that continuously resides there simply waiting to be acknowledged and called upon.

Our opportunities for healing and growth are continuous and infinite. Should we miss the opportunity to access this moment now, another moment immediately presents itself in the next now. But the trauma experiences holding our unresolved karmic lessons must, by the very nature of the space/time construct, connect directly to us across time and space in order to access the mind of God through our present now.

It is only now in this moment that we have come to this realization. This truth was hidden from us in the past buried within and beneath the weight of our own karmic burdens; burdens that we were then attempting to escape from at every distractive opportunity, even while attempting to enlist the help and support of some other person- who is really just another aspect of our former self oblivious to our own unique lessons.

These are the echoes across time that reach us now in this moment in the guise of unmanageable emotional feelings disrupting our comfort in the moment, leading to long practiced but entirely counter-productive coping mechanisms learned while very young, and crying out for healing; a healing that only we in the now can access by connecting back into the mind of God and accessing the unconditional love that resides there.

Rather than projecting our pain, anger and disappointment from these uncomfortable feeling moments outwardly towards others, it is now possible to distinguish ourselves from our past, recognize the voice of the child or younger person calling out to us from within our past, and express the love we access from our higher self in this moment directly back to the source of our discomfort in the past. It is this distinction that breaks away our karmic chains and completely changes the dynamic effects of our memories. The pain of abandonment, guilt and victimhood- and even the anger of innocent rage- is replaced with understanding and compassion, and the spiritual part of our real being is elevated to a higher vantage point upon our journey through life.

Remission of Sins

I do not call myself a born-again Christian, but I have a deep and sincere appreciation for the power of divine forgiveness as is practiced within orthodox Christianity. Regardless of whether the

Jesus of the Bible was born, lived and ascended as written, I have no doubt that the Christ Consciousness, the consciousness of pure unconditional love, exists and lives on.

And it was this consciousness that the said Jesus sought to teach and share with his disciples. In order for Christians to access and benefit from the remission of sins, it is absolutely necessary that the new Christians believe wholeheartedly in the love and power of Christ. Otherwise the aspect of forgiveness is empty and without substance. In the Christian sense, it has always been the love of Jesus and God that justifies forgiveness of sins and the resolution of karmic debts; which are basically the same things described by differing semantics.

Deepak Chopra's findings concerning the two-step process of remarkable recovery seem to confirm that real healing can and does occur on two distinct levels, perhaps either concurrently, or independently.

On the one hand, resolving the unresolved emotional trauma is obviously very powerful, especially when divine guidance is at hand.

On the other hand, faith and belief alone seem to be able to access healing and wholeness, especially when that faith approaches the threshold of 'knowing-ness' wherein there is no longer any doubt at all about who or what really runs the show.

To accept and believe in the power of love is an immensely powerful medicine whichever religion or spiritual teacher applies it. Because God is ageless and eternal, forgiveness, if accepted, has the power to cross the boundaries between time and space; even cancelling out old karmic debts resulting from unresolved 'sins' or, past life issues.

Once we begin to accept and fathom the ageless and eternal nature of God, it becomes clearer that all things are perfectly orchestrated even from the beginning of time until the end of time; that all times, places, and people are closely linked in the moment to the mind of God; and consequently that we are capable of linking up with every prior or later moment in our lives through this same mind of God.

Enter then the wounded child within who is directly communicating with us in our adult body from his/her own past 'now' through a time/space warp in the eternal mind of God. To heal that wounded child requires the same level of belief in the actual reality of that child, the eternal nature of God, and the infinite power of God's love, as born-again Christians rely upon in accessing their own forgiveness of sins through the power of Jesus Christ and the God from which he acquired his authority.

We need not believe in the doctrine of Christ, but in the power from which all doctrine emerged. And in this instance, simply believing in and acknowledging the reality of a real living child within crying out for love, gives one the perfect foundation and tools of faith to sincerely give that child exactly what she or he needs and deserves. Believe, and love, and you shall be made whole.

**The symbol of Infinity and the connectivity
of all people, times and places.**

The Power of Music

Curiously, part and parcel of my final healing involved music. At about the same time that I discovered and began loving my abandoned child within I also renewed my interest in music.

I borrowed a guitar and quickly learned anew how to strum a few tunes. Something truly captured me in this endeavor and I have become a decent guitarist within the past few months. And as I play I sing.

The singing came slowly at first, as I was weak and tenuous. Gradually I began to find my voice and experience music in an entirely new way. Finally it struck me that I was singing love to my wounded child, and that child was singing back to me across time.

Since the beginning of time the beating of drums, chants and music of all kinds have been used in healing ceremonies. The rhythmic vibrations we create and respond to during such activity takes us back subconsciously to the peaceful hiatus of the womb when we were safely held and lulled within the comforting thrall of our mother's heartbeat. It is no great surprise, then, that music and rhythm continue to bring us relief from worry and stress, stabilizing the human metabolism as powerfully as any modern drug.

Repeatedly music and sound have been proved to either aid or disrupt growth and healing in all living things, depending largely on the frequency and intensity of the vibrations. That we humans have the means to seek out and choose the vibrations we experience - either environmental or circumstantial - speaks hugely to the perfection of the human manifestation. However, choice manifests as a wonderful tool only upon its appreciation. Until we recognize our opportunities they are lost to us.

Most small children are taught to be silent in their needs and in the expression of their emotions. Consequently we learn to internalize our emotions and hide away from the traumatic karmic lessons foisted upon us. This is normal, even if not natural; and often manifests later as a fear of public speaking and an inability or discomfort to sing or perform before an audience.

Sometimes it evidences as a general passive-aggressive response that avoids confrontation at any cost, relying on subtle retaliation by subterfuge. We lose our voice, so to speak; and in losing that we lose our ability to truly and deeply connect with our own higher self and with all others.

Through the appreciation of music we can take on a new surrogate mother that can temporarily relax us, soothing circumstantial fears, worries and loneliness. And this is a good thing. How bleak the world might seem without music. But it is only a temporary substitute for the real thing, which is a permanent connection to the divine vibrations of unconditional love.

We choose the music we like according to our own unresolved emotional bias. Some music resonates with our childhood wounds. When we are 'blue' we listen to the 'blues'. Sometimes we seek out spiritually uplifting music. When we feel unloved, we play love songs. And if we carry a burden of unresolved anger, heavy metal may be our music of choice.

In all these cases we seem to tune in to the vibrations of the music, or at least choose the music that is closest to our own inner 'tune'. Surely the soothing nature of music has eliminated or at least averted many an attempted suicide? By the same measure how much has militant and aggressive marching music contributed to the deaths of millions in war?

Music can be constructive, healing or destructive, just as any tool or technology can be used or abused by its user.

What is even more powerful in the healing game is to become a music-maker. Learn to play an instrument and join others in the expression of rhythm and music. Connecting with others through music is not the be-all and end-all of such connection, but it can be a good start towards the powerful and empowering development of your own true voice - and your connection with others.

Learning to sing is an optimum medium for growth of the soul, and in learning how to find your voice. We all have a voice - and a message - but few are they who have the self-belief and courage to exercise that voice after years of being stifled and muzzled by our parents, families, teachers, caregivers and peers.

Singing becomes the ultimate vehicle for the expression of our deep and hidden emotions. And singing with another or with others brings us all even closer in resonance with the divine and with each other. Singing allows us to unburden ourselves at least temporarily from our troubles and to express our emotions from deep within.

One has only to listen to the compositions of Mozart or Beethoven to appreciate the timelessness of music. Such music projects across the centuries to express the genius of our other selves. Today we can still be moved by the age-old message that music brings. Perhaps music is the ultimate medium with which to communicate across the bridge of time?

You may have been fortunate enough to have had as an infant a mother, nanny or caregiver who sang to you to soothe and quieten your discomfort. Such lullabies are from an ageless tradition whose results have been tried and tested.

If you should find it difficult to reach out to your wounded child with pure and unconditional love, sing or play to him or her. Attach your love to the vibrations of music and song you create, and project that love directly to the place within where your child calls out to you for healing.

Your love and your song is as powerful as an atomic bomb. Even more so if you bring forth your emotional genius and write a song expressly for that wounded child. Nothing can be more personal or more effective than your personal love letter set to music, nor can anyone play or sing it better than you.

The song and the music becomes the perfect harmony when you intentionally align your vibrations to heal that lost and hurting child who is calling out to you.

It's Never too Late to Heal

As we pass through our life, our unresolved karmic lessons speak ever more loudly to us through the wounded child within. This message is first delivered in the form of mental conflict, begging us to simplify and resolve the incongruity between our sense of guilt, impending abandonment, and/or low self-worth; and the other emerging sense of innocent rage and/or victimhood.

Most 'normal' people choose one aspect or the other as the stage upon which they perform. Their personality then projects through the various coping mechanisms they developed as a child to help them survive their foundational abuse trauma; constantly reinforcing itself through predictable self-fulfilling expectations.

For those persons, the resolution of their childhood traumas is accomplished by first addressing the primary issue, and then using the same tools of discovery in moving on to the secondary.

Observe, own and resolve through love.

Some persons never achieve this level of emotional rebalancing, and consequently suffer through their life with one form or another of a mental imbalance mirroring the unresolved conflict between their own perceived guilt <u>and</u> innocence. This can manifest as phobias, manias, ADD, ADHD, bipolar disorder (formerly manic depressive illness), schizophrenia or a host of other mental dysfunctions; each making wholeness and wellness more difficult to access and experience.

In effect, these persons continue to try and be the two separate entities that they defined themselves to be as infants. Unless and until they are able to choose one aspect or the other to observe and resolve with their own innate higher intelligence, they will likely never be happy or healthy individuals. Such individuals rarely thrive, and often end their lives early through the slow death of institutionalism, trauma-instigated terminal illness, overt insanity and/or suicide.

Most normal persons continue to take with themselves the coping mechanisms they developed as a child, projecting those same behavioral patterns in all their relationships in life, whether they be in the work sector or in the more intimate relationships between friends and lovers. Those coping mechanisms then manifest in their lives whenever something happens that is similar to the original traumas experienced as a child.

Usually, the individual shies away from the new experience, using the original coping mechanism for protection. Invariably, that childhood coping mechanism will bring about the very outcome that the adult does not want to happen.

With time, the individual 'learns' through experience to avoid all such persons, places, or situations likely to recreate the childhood emotion; and consequently avoids revisiting that emotional place at all cost in order to avoid suffering the same emotional consequences. This ensures that the karmic lesson held within the emotion is rarely addressed, and consequently even more rarely healed.

Unfortunately, such is the nature of karmic balancing, that the universe will ensure that the lesson will present itself again and again until it is resolved, the lesson learned, and the gift of compassion is accepted and added on to our wisdom base.

As we pass through life, the wounded child within crying out for love and healing becomes ever more insistent and compelling in his or her need. Possibly that child within knows intuitively that we each must work against an ever-approaching use-by date in order to resolve our lessons lest we be required to re-confront the same challenges in our next lifetime.

What originally began as a mental conflict between our perceived guilt and like perceived innocence first became a minor personality dysfunction, then morphed into a serious and seemingly permanent personality dysfunction as the universe continued to present the lesson to us in varied forms. Later in life, even more pressing traumas raised the ante considerably; often manifesting as life threatening illnesses and diseases requiring our whole attention in order to resolve the foundational emotions involved.

What all these traumas and conflicts have in common is the natural human tendency to run away from the pain in order to avoid it. In fact, most persons spend their entire life running from their emotional past. Thus they never resolve it, ensuring that the same game plan will of necessity be in place next time around.

The karmic answer is always the same. Turn and face your worst fears. What are your worst fears? It's simple. Pain. Pain and more pain. We run from pain. We run from emotional pain in exactly the same way that we avoid physical pain. In a karmic sense there is no difference between the two. We delude ourselves in supposing that physical pain is more real and damning than emotional pain.

In truth, it is the emotional pain that kills more surely. Physical pain is easy to identify, and thus resolve; whereas emotional pain rarely reveals its true self, its origin, or any easy cure.

There is a good reason why there are actually very few death bed recoveries in the context of modern medicine. This is because once a disease situation begins to become painful, the patient almost always requests, and is given, a good dose of painkiller to alleviate the pain. In terms of deep and/or permanent healing this is exactly the worst possible medicine.

This ensures that the patient will have lost the means to embrace the foundational trauma which is now screaming out for healing almost with its last breath. The wounded child within is dying with the adult; an adult who no longer has ears to hear, and is probably also beyond caring.

Remarkable recoveries more often manifest long before the pain threshold is crossed and the patient succumbs to the temptation of pain killers and morphine. At this stage in the onset of the lesson (manifestation of the disease) the patient is still quite lucid and in control of his/her full faculties; and at least has the means to observe, own, and resolve the emotional issues underlying the disease condition.

Once the pain begins it is all the more difficult to take on the new emotional approach required to resolve the trauma, heal the wounded child inside, and own the whole circumstances of the disease. Physical pain is extremely distracting in the best of times. Consequently, owning one's pain in the grips of a diagnosed terminal disease, is not only difficult, it is also extremely rare.

However, this does not in any way remove the lingering possibility of karmic resolution through either a new and complete belief in the power of love, healing, and forgiveness; or, taking the very courageous approach of owning and surrendering oneself to the pain that is now expressing through and from the wounded child within. It continues to be your wounded child's pain that is manifesting in your body through your disease, just as it was previously your wounded child's emotional pain before the onset of the disease.

If you can observe and own the physical pain as your inner child's, surrender yourself entirely to the observation of that pain as being separate from that part of you that is doing the observing, and then open your own floodgates of love back to the suffering child within, it is still possible to regain wholeness of mind, body, and spirit and emerge reborn in every way.

What is not widely or commonly understood is that to the divine spirit, being everything and nothing simultaneously, every experience in physicality brings with it a form of divine ecstasy. And at the highest level of human consciousness every physical sensation, whether pain or pleasure, brings with it an experience in the bliss of being.

Every experience manifests from out of the mind of God, playing like divine music upon an otherwise blank musical score. And just as the pause defines the preceding music, the musical notes before the pause define it, too. All experience emits from out of the mind, heart, and soul of God. And love is all there is in God. Thus, at the core of all pain lies only unconditional love.

The more painful and 'lost' to the disease the pilgrim may be, the more joyous and celebratory all the angels in heaven when any person loves and trusts the perfect God enough to accept the 'now' in all its painful circumstances; which then opens the floodgates of divine love and healing. The crippled child within can then throw aside the crutches and dance in gratitude and delight.

The secret here is to accept, believe, and know that the pain you are feeling in your terminal illness is the unresolved pain of your wounded child within. That pain is manifesting in this way because you have spent a lifetime attempting to escape from it and the karmic responsibility associated with the unresolved lesson you have avoided thus far. In observing the pain, you automatically separate yourself from it, viewing it from the perspective of your higher self.

The pain is felt as your lower ego self refuses to divulge power and control to your higher self. It is the dissonance created by the conflict between your false illusion of self and your higher truth that has ultimately brought you to death's bed. And still, the only thing required of you in order to regain your spiritual health and wholeness is to first accept the disease and pain as a part of your own chosen process, surrender yourself completely to it and the lesson it holds, and then to love the pain and the wounded child experiencing it as wholly and purely as a father would love his dying child.

In this process one of two miracles will surely occur. The pain will transform itself away from its masquerade of discomfort, and reveal itself as pure and unconditional love. The wounded child will finally receive what he or she has been asking for and waiting for all these years. And you will likely be given the choice of continuing your journey towards a blissful form change back into the world of spirit, or to reclaim your physical health in order to complete your journey in physicality in comfort and wholeness.

Whatever your pain, be it physical or emotional, the cure is the same. Love your pain as the wounded child expressing it, and you and the child within will finally be transformed and released from your heavy burdens.

Our karma arrives as a specially prepared gift basket from heaven to assist us on our journey towards bliss.

But like winning a lottery ticket, karma must be owned and presented before the prize can be claimed.

The Genie in the Virus

All things emit from the Mind of God. All things are connected in God across time and space. There is a perfect order and reason in the cosmos.

What then about the viruses, bacterial diseases and cancers that plague society? Might they, too, take their marching orders from the Perfect God? Of course they do. Nothing else makes sense. They live and grow according to God's perfect word, just as every cell in our own bodies does, and just as we do.

Such elements are part of God's perfect plan of karmic learning, forcing home the karmic lessons that we in our ignorance refuse to accept graciously. Each pathogenic agent carries with it a message across time directly connecting with and from our unresolved past issues. There is a thread within these agents that connects with our childhood wounds and continues back through time right to the birthplace of our karma; the other selves that we have somehow injured or damaged in a past life.

And even as humankind in our ad hoc dance of survival strives to deny these karmic lessons through invasive surgery, radiation, chemotherapy, new antibiotics, and ingenious new diagnosis techniques, God continues to force our karmic lessons home by evolving new forms of karmic carriers; all the while patiently waiting for us to become all we came to be, or to simply be returned to the karmic wheel of life, God's own recycling bin.

This is why and how DNA in cells can change. When we accept and embrace our karmic lessons, we change the nature of our DNA, all those defective or infective cells carrying our karma suddenly become redundant to God's plan, and we experience spontaneous remission. This truly is the hand of God which we can exercise for and with God simply by accepting our gifts of karma. Sometimes this happens in a moment, and sometimes over a period of time.

Medicine will never understand or accept this concept unless or until humankind should one day discover how to identify and measure the pure energy of love. I'm not holding my breath for such a day.

Courage to meet and greet our worst fears begets miracles in a very scientific way. And Karma arrives as diamonds disguised as pain and disease.

It appears to me that modern medicine has become a kind of mathematics of fear. Ignorance minus love equals fear. Fear of death and fear of life.

Life without love. This is worse than death, tasting of eternal damnation. But don't worry. This too is only a passing illusion readily surrendered in the face of love. Are you ready to be loved?

What is Time?

Time is a continuum dependent upon space and movement for its perception and appreciation. Space plus movement creates the experience of time passing. The fabric of the universe is often called a space/time continuum, in that neither can exist nor be perceived independently of the other. Both are part of the majestic illusion of creation. In order for us to perceive ourselves as something within time and space we must buy into the illusion that we are not something else – the other somethings.

Thus begins the belief that we are separate from God – and also separate from all other things, places, peoples and times outside of our own singular moment-space.

The 'now' is as much a place as a time; in fact encompassing all time and space.

Only by traveling through the illusion of time and space in a linear manner can we appreciate and experience the breadth and scope of Divine Mind. The space-time continuum is the showcase of all creation. Without time there can be no movement and nothing to 'show'; and without space there is no place to show it.

Time and space create the stage upon which Divine Mind plays through us. We chose our parts, but often forget our lines. God waits in the wings to prompt us when all else fails; provided we share the credits. If we are not looking in his direction we are likely to lose the plot.

The wise man looks and moves towards God with singular purpose and vision, and ultimately arrives at his destiny. In bliss.

From within chaos there is an ultimate end, and a new beginning, for divine order. Science has identified a unifying order to all things which perpetually rebirth themselves. This order is manifesting at every level of creation. Atoms, living systems, solar systems, galaxies, even the cosmos- is in process of perpetually destroying and recreating itself.

This divine order of death and renewal is called the torus. This is particularly evident in the world of nature wherein nature perpetually feeds upon itself.

There is not a single particle, energy or movement in the universe that was not born out of an intentional forgetfulness in the mind of God while the torus continues to play itself out.

The torus represents the karmic wheel of life, to which we almost always must return. However, because we hold the key to Godhood within ourselves as the very essence of our life, once we release ourselves from all our karmic bonds and accept our role as co-creators of the cosmos we are able to stand beside God in bliss for all eternity.

It is my forgetfulness, the ego, now accepted and chosen as the perfect vehicle of existence, that has blessed me with richness, adventure and diverse experience in my life. I now seek a life of refined balance.

To remember, but still allow myself to forget a little. To forget a little but not forget to remember. I believe this is the secret to eternal life. To continue to narrow the path of ego until we are able to stand fully in God's glory even as the angels do.

Remembering and forgetting. The yin and yang of duality, and the primary recipe for all creation.

Every Diamond has a Flaw
& so do We

The many human flaws that we try to correct in our lives may very well be the foundation of our experiences. We must be separate from the source - imperfect - before we can experience any aspect of it. Our sense of separation is the basis for all our human frailties. Because we believe we are disconnected from God, this leads on to our sense of unworthiness, guilt, anger and innocent rage. In a way, the more separated and broken we may feel, the more likely it is that we will seek out a higher intelligence and strive to reconnect with our source.

Thus, imperfection is the foundation of all experience. Experience is the stuff of divine entertainment. We create the quality of our experience with, by, and for God by our own choices. Enlightenment is the process by which our choices, and thus our experiences, lead on to bliss rather than discomfort, pain and suffering. Imperfection is the game board upon which we strive- with divine guidance through karma- to achieve an eternal state of bliss.

Step by step, we can love our humanness almost into submission, accept all our unresolved karmic lessons, and move as close to God as our growing self-worth permits moment by moment.

The ultimate challenge is to resolve as many of our self-imposed judgments against our imperfection as we can while still retaining enough of our flawed humanness in order to observe God and all her creation from a distance. That is the only way we can see God. That is the only way we can attain an eternal existence. It is also the only way God can see, experience, and enjoy us- in apparent separation- and at a distance.

Even from the beginning of time we emerged from nothingness and chose to be something by separating ourselves from everything else.

Through our many lives we give up our sense of separation only little by little so as to not fall completely back into the non-being of 'everything' and become nothing again. It is the separation of God from itself that brings forth the illusion and experience of all creation.

We are all in process of recycling back towards God. It is a wonderful and entertaining journey. As we move closer and closer to God, the path of ego – which is separation - narrows more and more. This is the cost of bliss. It is the surrendering up of our egoistic physical identity to which we have become attached through our many lifetimes.

In order to attain perfection, we must give up all that is not perfect. If we gave up our entire ego what would we have left upon which to stand? Surely we would disappear once again into the non-experiential energy of the great something-nothing of God.

There must be something perfect held within ego that gains us access to everlasting life and bliss.

Perhaps the secret to everlasting life is to remove our human mask and simply identify ourselves not as something separate from God, but rather as the pure but unique expression of the divine that we are. By discovering our uniqueness, our own special genius, we pass the test of perfection. We can be God, and by our uniqueness stand beside her as well. Forever.

Because straight is the gate, and narrow is the way, which leadeth unto life, and few there be that find it.

Matthew 7, v.14

213

The Earth: A University for Angels

I've often heard it said by deeply spiritual individuals that life is simply a type of school for spiritual development. The question that always came up for me was, 'School for what? What happens when we graduate? What is the other thing or place that this life is preparing us for?'

It finally came to me, and only recently when I finally unhitched my karmic chains and began flying. This life is a school for angels. That's it!

Life, with all its drama, karma, dharma and lessons is a proving ground, a refining ground, and a playground for us forgetting children of God. The only way we or anyone can truly appreciate what we (and God) are is to forget ourselves enough to perceive the glory of God in separation, and to remember ourselves enough to know that there is something to forget. But before we can attain that level of consciousness, we must proceed upon the wheel of karma in order to experience, learn, and know how to be in God's perfect love; how to express it, how to communicate it, and how to be it.

Nothing else will do.

I am now totally in love with God, life, and myself and have finally freed myself from my karmic chains. Life has quite suddenly become a new angelic realm for me, blessing me with unimaginable beauty, tear jerking wisdom and insight, and an unflappable connective fiber to all persons, places and things.

This truly is a Paradise that I have become competent enough to gain entrance to; simply by giving up my reliance and dependence upon my past, and accepting my unique divinity. It's always been right here waiting for me to wake up. I have become an angel on to myself and a ministering angel to all whom I meet in love.

My new excitement at life can scarcely be touched upon by this book; but the book is the first tangible expression of that new vibration that I attune myself to each moment.

Throughout the universe, the source is constantly creating new worlds, and peopling them with new souls. In order for new souls to learn the truth and meaning of life, it is necessary for them to engage upon the karmic wheel of life, first being the darkness, and then experiencing the darkness in order to learn compassion, the real reason for being, and the only way to 'be' in love.

We live in a relatively new world; one that has not yet globally ascended onto the evolutionary angelic realm. Even though we continue to slaughter each other in countless wars around the world- as we must in order to learn who or what we are not- there is a new consciousness gradually manifesting behind that turning wheel of karma. Slowly but surely, we are beginning to get it.

After each new slaughter there are a few reincarnated souls that take the lessons and grow with them. They learn that there's more to life than murder and butchery. And very soon there will be enough new angels in our world to provide a global lift-off of sorts, allowing the entire population of the earth to ascend en masse to reveal a very real heaven on earth; one that already exists for those precocious souls who have already discovered their angel wings and realized the joy of connecting with the one great mind, the one great soul, and the one great heart of God.

This is ultimate love. That's all there is and all there will ever be.

All around the world, more and more people are talking about, and making, a connection with their higher self. We live in an exciting time, the ever-present 'now'. The place where everything is happening and the only place where anything happens.

Imagine the world of mankind to be like a very large and complex jig-saw puzzle, with all the pieces mixed and scattered in every land. Imagine that each of these puzzle pieces has a side that connects to all others, and a side that connects to no other.

Each of those pieces that imagine themselves to be their circumstances, the false identity of the ego, separate themselves from all others by hiding their connective edges and revealing their non-connective edges defined by the ego. The ego is the creation of an illusion based upon the result of all that we have done, experienced, or achieved. While we believe in our ego self, we are beyond connection with our true higher self, and we are beyond connection with others.

Thus our relationships are seldom close or deep, as our ego creates a barrier to true connection. We rarely trust others to give us what we need, and we are rarely trusted. Under most circumstances the ego behaves like a noisy watchdog guarding the heart, chasing away anyone who comes close by. Real love can simply not get in.

Each of those puzzle pieces that have discovered their true self above and beyond their ego learn to present their beautiful connective parts to the world, being easily connectable to all others who present with a desire to connect in love. Now, what is happening in the world is that groups of individuals are beginning to discover their true connective nature. Couples are beginning to connect on a truer and deeper level. Individuals are beginning to relate with others in the expression of love and connection.

So, even in the midst of all the confusion in the world, we are beginning to see little clumps of connected pieces scattered amongst all the individual ones. In some places the clumps are becoming truly significant; perhaps hundreds or even thousands joined together. These clumps actually magnify the attractive nature of their individual components, and as the clumps grow larger they attract more and more individuals towards their connection, and an even more powerful vibrational energy is created. And via the internet we are seeing connective fibers beginning to span the globe in cyber-space.

This appears to be the start of something huge. Soon, little clumps will fit together to become bigger clumps, and bigger clumps will connect together to become even bigger clumps. And just as we sometimes complete a jig-saw puzzle by joining together already connected pieces, we are creating a tapestry of connection around the world which will one day connect us all in a magnificent world of love and connection. The movement towards connection is already unstoppable.

One day very soon, permission and acceptance will rule, negativity will be the exception, and charity will be the principal means of exchange. We may still need money, but we will use it not to control each other, but as another way of loving and sharing.

We first learn who we are not. Then who we might be. It must be so, for there are no other choices.

Bliss is a choice, even if it is a last choice.

Money as an Angelic Means of Sharing

The secret of happiness and good health lies in owning our karma. That means taking the lesson no matter how it arrives, however painful, and from whomever. In a nutshell, this also means owning our feelings entirely, without projecting them onto others, or feeling ourselves to be the victim.

This is total self-responsibility.

In the angelic realm of the near future, we will also become totally self-responsible for our own economic well being. That is, for the supply of everything that we need in order to pursue life and worship in love.

There is one relatively simple and easy change to our present economic paradigm that may by itself be the major catalyst for the coming global ascension. That is, the elimination of all taxation. Then again, it may come about because of the global ascension. Whatever the case may be, I have chosen to ascend now, and then see what happens later. This book is an expression of my own expansion. We live in exciting times.

At present all money is created by self-serving interests intent in gaining control over this world of journeying souls. This new money, being created out of thin air in cyber-space, is then sold into circulation through a carefully constructed banking system as interest-bearing debt.

Part and parcel of this economic system is the false belief that taxes must be extracted in order to fund government services and provide some sort of welfare state for the less fortunate. In general, it is taxes that force private individuals to surrender their property ownership rights over to the banking industry in order to obtain the new money needed to pay their taxes. And the banking industry obtains their money at interest from the real money masters in cyber space.

The curious truth is taxes are the very thing that prevents government and economic systems generally from operating in a sustainable way.

Even on the face of it, it's clear that there can never be enough money (principle) to repay principle plus interest. This is a mathematical impossibility. As well, taxes provide a distinct disincentive to create wealth, and become heavily parasitic on the creative energy available within an economic system.

In addition, taxes, and the perceived poverty consciousness that results, lead to an ever widening gap between the rich and the poor. Taxation also creates the illusion of shortage of wealth, and a very real shortage of money.

The shortage of money drives up interest rates favoring the wealthy and disadvantaging the poor even more. There has never been a fair system of taxation and there never will be. Taxes amount to a grand cosmic fraud, and are undoubtedly a part of our karmic journey of learning what and who we are not. They certainly are proving what does not work in obtaining fairness and connective oneness for all beings.

This is a carefully constructed conspiracy created by a core group of egocentric souls in forgetfulness, so far successfully deluding the masses into accepting a system that is systematically taking ownership over all worldly assets and all nations. For us to increase our wealth and business base (and theoretically improve our quality of life) we must give away the ownership of our assets in order to borrow the new money needed to pay our taxes and to service the interest portion of our debts.

The present system ensures that the better part of humanity will become and remain slaves to debt until this system is universally upturned.

In the angelic realm of the future, every soul will own every aspect of his/ her own well-being. Every soul will be and know that they are absolutely responsible for their own choices and outcomes. And every soul will be given precisely what they need in order to continue their karmic journey towards ultimate enlightenment and fulfillment in love.

In truth they already are, but this is hidden under an avalanche of propaganda and lies meant to convince us that we are slave to our present circumstances and the power structures that presently exist.

The major difference will be that we will all be able to spend a much greater part of our spiritual life engaged in love and loving rather than dealing with old unresolved karmic lessons, as we are in the present time. As well, every soul will be immediately rewarded with every fruit of their own labors.

This is how it will work:

What gives money value in the present system is the relationship between wealth and debt. Because all money comes into being as an interest bearing debt, all money is debt and all debt is money. Changing the relationship between wealth and money (debt) changes the value of the money.

At present, the debt/money supply is increasing faster than the wealth supply. In truth, when considering the degradations of the environment, it may well be that our real wealth base is declining even as the money supply increases. This is being reflected in the inflationary trend whereby money is generally becoming less and less valuable and soon will be attaching to itself higher and higher interest rates. This further widens the gap between the rich and the poor.

Wealthy speculators profit handsomely both in an inflationary system and in boom and bust cycles that destroy the middle classes and those below. Those on fixed or passive incomes such as pensioners fall behind during inflation, seeing their incomes and savings slowly being whittled away; and those who are heavily in debt lose their businesses and homes during times of high inflationary interest rates, or when the equities in their homes disappear during a depression.

The rich are always Johnny on the Spot to pick up, and own the resulting temporarily devalued pieces.

Should, however, the wealth base increase faster than the money supply, the value of money will increase unless more money enters the system. This is the key to the New Angelic Order of Economics. In the absence of taxation, individuals will take more ownership over their own energies, applying them more diligently, and creating a larger personal wealth estate.

As the wealth estate held by private persons increases, the enlightened service government of the future will simply increase the money supply to match the new wealth created by the private interests.

Thus all government services will be paid for with new interest-free money, and the value of money will remain relatively fixed and stable, encouraging long term investment rather than speculative opportunity.

In addition, because the private sector will provide far more of its needs in future than at present under the present system, government will have the admirable responsibility and requirement to distribute untold billions of dollars directly to the citizens of the nation as a universal benefit guaranteeing that every single person will own their circumstances, their opportunities and their dreams.

And the more successful a single individual becomes in the economic sense, the more opportunity that individual gifts the state in the introduction of a comparable amount of money to the general citizenry.

This is divine charity as it is meant to be.

The concept of personal ownership of our circumstances is the single driving force held within the entire universe. This is what makes the universe and all in it evolve. We are all totally responsible for our own being, our own experiences, our own feelings, and all our own circumstances.

The God in me owns itself in every way, shape, and form. And we are all gods. Why would it be any different in the economic world of man, except in his present painful but karma-enlightening forgetfulness?

When will this new paradigm take hold?

How will that happen?

Sorry, but we do have a little way to go, and I may be getting ahead of myself.

Money: neither a means nor an end, but an alluring and seductive mistress all the more compelling in its elusiveness.

Taxes: the means by which Samson is shorn of his power and his freedom.

EPITAPH TO TAXES

Here lie taxes dead and buried,
No more bullies, none to pay.
Some think life and love are ended,
Society in disarray

Of life and love I spare no thought for,
Till my people are well fed.
Many suffer from lack of love,
But also from a lack of bread.

Nations grow through real things made,
Not by sharing one pie further.
Help the baker make a second,
Buy his pie, he'll bake another.

Where does money go we query,
Scattered from our hand asunder?
Maybe we should ask ourselves,
From where it comes, we ought to wonder.

What is government, you ask?
It is we and we are it.
The less it has to do for us,
The more we keep, the more we get.

If you tax a man to death,
He works no more so save your breath.
Tax him just a little less,
He may still live, but what a mess!

How difficult it is for you,
To let him keep his hard earned wages,
Just try it once, you'll be surprised,
You'll see his savings grow in stages.

If he saves beyond his needs,
The extra stuff is his to sell.
Government can buy those things,
By printing money, can't you tell?

People then will have enough
And will not need to be so tough,
In grabbing more than what they need
While watching poorer people bleed.

Charity will win the day.
And poverty will be at bay.
We will love and never fear,
And paradise will be right here!

Here lie taxes dead and buried,
They are gone and we are well,
Where they are now I can't answer,
But I think they've gone to hell.

DARE TO CONNECT

There is a crack in heaven, that's how the light gets in.
Illuminates just where we are and where in past we've been.
Some see it through the darkness, some hear it as a sound.
Some feel it as amazing grace and know that they've been found.

I hear it as a ringing that wakes me from my sleep.
A long lost contract I have made that I am bound to keep.
But even then I'm not complete, there's still a missing part.
That I can only find myself by opening my heart.

That's when true vision comes to me and I begin to see
That I can love another and, that is the way to 'be.'
Perhaps you are that other me that I've been looking for;
The missing piece that I can't see when I myself explore.

Connection only happens when the three become the one;
When we and God combine we then can have some serious fun.
Connection is the thing that makes the universe go round.
And even though we may be linked it doesn't make us bound.

We have a choice in all we do, how far we want to go.
And when we do connect, how much we want to show.
Until we understand our fate, which is ourselves to know,
We'll keep on looking elsewhere, and in circles we will go.

This is the karmic wheel of life upon which we all sit.
Until we find completion we are bound to stay on it.
We can't connect with anyone, until we find our self.
When we succeed upon that task we've finally found true wealth.

For once we know we are complete within our earthly being,
Our senses are expanded, which leads us to more seeing.
Our eyes can then express our truth, not taking but in giving,
In seeing with our higher self, we can rejoice in living.

To first connect with self opens doors of true belonging,
Which then connects to others to satisfy our longing.
We can't connect until we set aside our false perception;
That we might be our circumstance is quite a misconception.

That simply is our ego which is based upon our past.
Until we learn to let it go, to us it will hold fast.
Observe your ego, it's not hard, in all your circumstance,
To see it is to own it which creates a special dance.

Your ego is your tool box, and really, nothing more,
It helps you navigate your life, and move from shore to shore.
Your memories are valuable, a treasure chest in fact,
To know the thoughts that do not serve preserves the 'now' intact.

The ego gives us wheels to roam until we find our place,
That's always ready there for us, no matter what our pace.
And gives a place to start from till we're ready then to fly.
And once we do, it's easy; come on and give a try!

To know the past is helpful to see from where we've come,
To understand how far we've come, and know what's still undone.
The past can cloud the perfect now; the now, then, can't be seen.
You can't go back, just try it; you will know just what I mean.

And yet there may be karma caused by what we did before,
In our past life before we entered this life's newfound door.
As children we all paid our debt, it wasn't ever fun,
Because of that we are now free, no need to now run from.

We simply need to go on back and feel the pain once more,
Accept it as our very own and know it's ours for sure.
Be brave and face your karmic debt, a moment is enough,
The prize is yours when you face up, it's just a judgment bluff.

There isn't any punishment for anything we've done,
There simply is a lesson that we already have won.
There isn't any other soul that we have hurt in past,
We sinned against our self perhaps and that's what makes it last.

Accept your fate and move ahead, it's time to let things go,
It's owning all our karma that permits us then to grow.
When we accept our karma this leads on to understanding;
That those we hurt are really us, it's truly quite demanding.

It's karma gives the angels the wings by which they fly,
And lets you give your trauma true permission then to die.
So put your karma in its place, the real you in control,
Wear your captain's hat and you will go where you would go.

Connection needs commitment that you stay upon the course,
Until you truly find yourself and know that you are source.
And in that space you will belong to all and they to you,
And love will grow between yourselves no matter what you do.

When you connect to your true source, you'll know you're not alone,
You'll be connected to all things and know that you are home.
Dare to connect to source, you're worthy I am sure,
Trust me when I say that you are absolutely pure.

The real you is connectable to persons, places, things,
The false you is the worry thoughts that ego always brings.
Your higher self waits patiently within your silent mind,
You only need to listen there and you will surely find.

You are *the universal mind just waiting to be heard,*
And everything you have in life emits from out your word.
It isn't overpowering, you needn't pay attention.
But if you do and find yourself it's really worth a mention.

Because therein there lies the mystic sounds of all creation.
And when one listens with one's heart it leads to true elation.
Seven sounds will call to you, it is the siren's song,
And when they merge as one, you surely will belong.

This is one grand connection for which we came to life,
To know ourselves as order in the midst of endless strife.
No longer listening to the sounds but with them being one,
You are *the Mind of God, and thus, your life has just begun.*

You are the silence listening to what you have put out,
It's seeing through the eyes of man is just what God's about.
When any two perceive this truth within and then do meet,
The magic sees itself in each and knows it is complete.

This is the Universal Soul, again in love, requited.
We once were two and now we're one, to love once more admitted.
It turns itself from inside out revealing all its glory,
All mystery and magic are woven in the story.

This is a grand fulfillment throughout eternity,
To see my own reflection in another perfect me.
This is the mighty soul of God laid bare for us to see.
The universe and all it holds I see ourselves to be.

And what is it that I might see when you permit me to?
The universe and all it holds I see inside of you.
I bring with me the Mind of God, so you, too, understand,
That I can't be complete unless with me you too will stand.

Bring then your eyes and ears of God to touch my naked breast,
Then let your body merge with mine and we are truly blessed.
There is but one such body now, it is the newborn Christ,
Within which we are all the same, you shouldn't be surprised.

This is the body of the Christ we feel through our one heart,
The Heart of God it is I feel, the Christ I know thou art.
Our Bodies, Minds, and Souls converge, this is the Trinity,
That God pursues at every chance throughout eternity.

We are all Gods, with this great gift, to love with no condition.
I dare you to connect, for Connection is our mission.

I HAD A DREAM 9/11 2001

In the dream, the world seemed to crumble around me, and I thought of you.
The earth moved, tearing away all my old belief systems, and I thought of you.
I was in a hijacked airplane, and I knew I was going to die, and I thought of you.
Having accepted my death, in the brief moment before impact I thought of you.
Then I was in a tall building, surrounded by fire and confusion, and I thought of you.
We were burning, my friend and I, and as we realized we were going to die, I thought of you.
We joined hands and leaped out of the 104th floor window into eternity, and I thought of you.
Then I was above the fire, and I felt the building tremble beneath me, and I thought of you.
As the falling building engulfed me, I thought of you.
As I heard the news that my wife had been in the airplane, I thought of you.
As I heard that my husband had been working in the building, I thought of you.
As I sat in front of the TV and heard all the awful news, I thought of you.
Then my dream changed to a battle scene, and I thought of you.
Bombs were falling, and people all around were screaming, and I thought of you.
As a bullet entered my breast, I thought of you.
I died a thousand deaths, and always, you were there in my thoughts.
And then I awoke from the dream, and I thought of you.
But things seemed so strange, so still, so peaceful, that perhaps this too was a dream.
The sky was bluer, the flowers more vivid, the moment more precious, the thought of you even more wonderful. Surely, if this too is a dream, I choose to dream this dream.
But in all my dreaming, one thing has always remained the same. You were always there in my thoughts. The thought of you made dying, and living, easier. Thank you for loving me.

ADIEU

I'm not my past, not any more
The needy guy I was before.
You've helped me find in truth the door,
A better way to be, explore.

I hope you've learned this lesson, too,
It's love that makes life seem more true,
There's nothing that you need to do,
What's inside me is inside you.

But if you're not quite happy, still,
Not heaven found, yet, so you feel,
There's plenty time to find what's real,
Just call on love, and come, it will.

When all seems lost, and hope's away,
When I'm alone, and fear holds sway,
It's then I need on love to call,
So I won't any further fall.

Love always comes, it never fails
To honor me within my need,
And shows a way that I might grow
Providing food so soul might feed.

So don't despair, you're not alone.
There's nothing that you must atone.
Just simply ask for love to be
And in that love, please join me.

Now even though the past is gone
(Past feelings can't be held for long)
The moment always rings love's song;
It's to that ringing we belong.

The seven ringings call on you,
All through the night and all day too,
To rise above where you've come from
And see that your life's just begun.

In every challenge I go through,
I'm asked one question, 'Who are you?'
This book is just another clue,
So till we meet in love, adieu.

With all my love
Carl Peterson

About the Author

Carl with his daughter Leah and mother Ann
on her 100th birthday party

Carl presently lives in Tauranga, New Zealand, where he offers spiritual life coaching and in his leisure time plays tennis and the guitar as often as he can.

Carl's previous publications include *Earth Changes* (1998) where he explores the possibility and probability of a future polar shift and *The Spirit of Economics* (1998) which examines the counterproductive effects of income taxes. He followed this with *The Zen of No Tax* (2005) where he discusses the dynamics and benefits of a tax-free tax system.

Presently he assists his son Karl Jacob Peterson in building, developing and marketing the Weekend Warrior and Gladiator portable sawmills.